Don't think of a Black Cat...!

A Beginners Guide to NLP

Peter Wright

Acknowledgements

In the text of this book I have mentioned the many persons who have introduced me to a new way of thinking and of viewing the world. But it would be remiss of me not to give special thanks to a close and special group. Without them I would not have had the varying degrees of support necessary to reach this stage.

To my close family go the greatest thanks. They have endured my quest with me, even though it might not have been of their choosing and they have been there every inch of the way. Their unconditional support has been the greatest resource. Thanks also go to my many tutors and mentors, and especially Dr Adam Vile and Jo Biggs for their total enthusiasm, inspiration and generosity. To the great number of my fellow coaches, who have witnessed and shared with me some exhilarating moments in this great adventure and who must have wondered sometimes where I was going to and what I'd be saying next. To the constant and endless stream of athletes and sportspersons, my heartfelt thanks for your trust and for your most fulfilling feedback.

Writing this book has been an education and a labour of love for me. Getting it appraised and corrected required people with real skill and dedication. A special mention goes to Megan Ramsay for her invaluable proof reading expertise. Megan, like Adam, Jo, my son Asa and fellow coach Warren Carr, have all selflessly read, evaluated and ultimately made a large contribution to this project. Thanks to you all for your advice and encouragement.

© Copyright Peter Wright 2008

ISBN: 978-0-9561522-0-6

Foreword to 1st Edition

I am a sports coach, actively involved in cricket and rugby. I am also a specialist mental preparation and performance coach, both in sports and other key areas of performance in business, performing arts and social interaction. These involve using strategies associated with NLP, hypnosis and other areas of sports and human psychology. Many of the examples described in the book are taken from the sporting side of my work with clients, but the crossover of these strategies into general areas of application is of key importance to anyone looking to tackle many of the issues that can beset us in our daily lives.

When, some years ago, I set out to discover more about sports psychology, little did I know what a fascinating and interesting path I would be taking, and the manifold self transformations would take place along the way. Looking at those foothills from this point further up the mountain, at no point down there was there ever a consideration of my also doing general therapy, coaching coaches, or writing books. No-one said to me *then* "Trust your unconscious". Although more recently it has been said, both to and by me.

I spent some of those early coaching years working with Glyn Offield, a colleague and friend who was a huge inspiration to both me and to all who knew him. Glyn witnessed a number of my first forays and encounters with Zen moments in coaching, and always took them on board as being the norm rather than "off-the-wall". Also, for him, life was for living and about seizing the moment. He created a huge circle of fellowship just being himself. I'd like to dedicate this book to Glyn's enduring spirit.

TABLE of CONTENTS

Preface	7
Overview of Topics	15
Introduction	17
Part 1 Your Toolkit	27
Part 2 Using the Tools	55
Part 3 Fitting the Appliance	71
Additional Practical Exercises	93
Motivation Towards or Away	97
Goals & Well-Formed Outcomes	98
Conclusion	101
Glossary of Terms	103
Recommended Reading	105
Inspirational Acknowledgements	109

PREFACE

To Be Is Not To Be

When philosopher and scientist Alfred Korzybski coined his (now) famous quote, **"The Map is not the Territory"**, I wonder if he had any idea that 70+ years on some of his original thoughts and ideas would be having an effect on as many people as they have.

Considered by some as a crucial ancestor of NLP, Korzybski compared the statement "Joe is an idiot" (concerning a fictitious character, Joe, who has committed a crass act) with "Joe has done something idiotic". The first statement implies Joe is something of a simpleton while the second statement is all about some thoughtless act he has done. It is centred around the use of the verb *To Be* in language. In the case of **"The Map is not the Territory"** the distinction highlighted by the *To Be* reference (in this case it is *Is Not*) points directly towards a founding principle in NLP, hence its oft-quoted reference. You could extend this to **"The Team is not the Team Sheet"**, **"The Holiday is not the Brochure"** or more amusingly **"The Meal is not the Menu"**. Again, this hinges on the *Is Not* reference; mind you in some fast food establishments the menu (and what it is printed on) can be a distinct improvement on the meal!

The idea seems simple enough. Who, after all, would confuse a roadmap with a road, or a menu with a meal? Yet Korzybski observed that people often confuse what they think with reality. Korzybski also coined the term *neuro-linguistic*, referring to the connectedness of our nervous systems and physical responses to our thoughts as structured by the language we use.

So, let's roll out some of the MAPS Joe might have in his chart room:

> "I'm useless"
> "I never feel confident"

"No one ever listens to me"
"I'll never make it"

I'm sure you can think of many other generalisations like these, made over the years by you and other people.

But once you start to pose specific questions of these particular maps, these generalisations, then the picture changes.

"What evidence is there that tells you <u>that</u>?"
"You've never felt confident ever? Not at any time, about anything?"
"What no one listens, ever? Why, I'm listening now!"
"What makes you think you'll never make it?"

Now consider some of your own maps…especially those in areas where things always seem to hold you back; then start breaking them down by questioning the assumptions and generalisations. If you are totally objective you should start to feel differently about them. We all carry some limiting beliefs around with us and if they are traced back to origin we might be surprised where they came from! They are not always our own judgements, or those of our parents, or friends, colleagues, classmates, or teachers or coaches, either. They might even be attributable to some casual overheard remark by someone totally unqualified to make any such observations.

Without questioning them though, our lives continue their course with these distorted maps. When we then come to specific areas where we might be having difficulties, it is as if we then look at the maps, then look at the world around us, and our will and confidence inside just dissolves. "There, see? I knew I wouldn't be any good at it!" This reinforces the credibility of the maps and makes them equally relied upon and trusted the next time they are consulted. "I'm too old to learn new tricks"…limiting beliefs, **thus**, distorted maps.

Without questioning and if left to their own devices, our brains will accept whatever maps we give them and will use them again and again. They have a strong tendency, however, to re-use preferred maps, regardless of the territory. So, you might be undertaking a new task and your brain will go and search for a strategy (a map, a **PROGRAMME**) to assist with the task completion. However, imagine the outcome if the particular chosen map does not correspond to the territory you are navigating!

Chaos → disappointment → external ill-judgement → reduction of confidence or reinforcement of low self-esteem……not a very appealing path!

It would be as if someone moved to France from the UK but continued to use his UK roadmap because he was familiar with it and liked it better than the French roadmap. It sounds ludicrous but we all do something like that with our mental maps. Mainly because we often don't realise we are using a map at all.

Take the very organised, controlled person for instance. This map, strategy or programme for dealing with the world and other people would serve them particularly well if their job called for someone with these specific attributes. However, take this map into social and close relationships and it might not suit the situations anything like as well. Think of people you know who are like this, and I guess there are many, and then find yourself pondering how their life might be better, easier, improved if they had another behavioural map here. There are lots who do have a range of behavioural maps…and there are lots who don't!

NLP, Training and Preparation for Performance

NLP began in the mid–1970s in the USA with the work of John Grinder, a professor of linguistics, and Richard Bandler, a psychologist. They began by studying excellent communicators, building models of communication skills. These methods could then be modelled by and taught to others so they too could get the same results. This is rather along the lines where you would use a perfect exponent of a particular skill within your profession or sport as an illustration, and then model your actions upon that master.

NLP is really tailor-made for performers in whatever discipline because through the various stratagems (or models as they are known) you can learn and understand the reality of how the masters work, think and represent the world and their perception of it, and can match their various patterns accordingly to help *you* move towards and achieve *your* goals.

Neuro (logy) – The mind and how we think
Linguistics – How we use language and how it affects us
Programming – How we sequence our actions to achieve our goals

NLP also studies how we represent our subjective experiences, how our senses build our internal perception of the world, how we think about our values and beliefs, how we create our emotional states. NLP extends the definition of *'map'* to include all the above. The implications are profound. We can never know a thing in itself; we can only know our own neurological translation of it. By the time we are aware of anything through our senses, it has already undergone significant transformations. Information has been deleted, distorted and generalised by our nervous systems in the very process of performing what we call 'perception'. So, our view of reality has been processed in our sensory language, all of which will be different. Mine, yours, his, hers or theirs. As an individual, this information can be really beneficial in helping you understand yourself, what your various maps are and how they might be improved, and what the effects of good state management might bring for you.

As a team leader or member, you already know how important communication styles and language are in helping the team function better as a unit, how the team will have a better rapport and improve their interaction, and NLP will illustrate for you the means of enhancing these skills and competences. An astute manager will be able to communicate with the team in such a way that he or she is on the wavelength of all of them. An astute salesperson will be able to communicate with customers in such a way that reaps greater benefits. Astuteness does not come as standard. However, with even some knowledge and practiced use of NLP, you will find your understanding and influence of players, teams, groups and customers will be greatly enhanced and that your evolving team dynamic drives all members forward with congruence and increased potential for success.

What I will outline for you in this book are some core NLP models, strategies, thought-provoking scenarios and some other methods and techniques used in sports psychology. With practice and motivation, you can start to use these even at a very basic level. As you read and work through the exercises you will find the experience stimulating, liberating, motivating, and that it opens the door to furthering your enjoyment of performance, and with that enriching the lives and successes of you and your team whatever your discipline.

The key to integrating NLP into your everyday communication is to have and to hone a style that encourages everyone to improve their skills and competences through experience and perception; to understand what is happening to yourself and those around you; and to understand what you and they need to do, internally (neurologically) and externally (physiologically) to bring about change.

Remember these maxims:

- **People are not their behaviours**
- **There are no unresourceful people, only unresourceful states**
- **If it's possible in the world then it's possible for me. It's just a matter of how**
- **For things to change first I must change**

- **There is no failure only feedback**

The road to consistently successful performance is paved with good preparation and organisation. "Fail to prepare and you prepare to fail" is often quoted, and is a good mantra for motivation. But you can be the most diligent and motivated person in training but fail to spot that the maps that are your guide are faulty. It's true you can be well organised but when the kitchen is getting hot can you still turn out a soufflé or zabaglione, or will you burn the toast?

NLP and mental skills training will help you cope with yourself, and this book distils the range of topics into a series of practical guides and tips, plus exercises to expand your awareness and perception of both language and communication. It is designed to make you think and act and effect change for yourself and those around you.

THE "LAW of 21"

If you keep up with a new mindset and take action on it for 21 days in a row it will begin to become a habit. Your mind will become so accustomed to that behaviour that it will begin to accept it as second nature. So, the particular actions I recommend here, such as abdominal breathing, SMART goal setting, getting control of your state, enhancing your communication skills and sensory acuity and using visualisation. They all fall under the Law of 21.

As with all transformation and change your positive involvement is vital. It won't just happen for you. You will have to work at it, but it will be worth it! The ratio of preparation to performance should be akin to an iceberg. All the prep is below the surface. The duck glides smoothly across the water, while below the legs are paddling furiously.

You will find how important questions are within NLP. Questions that challenge maps, over generalisations and unconsidered opinions. The question is, are you ready to make all the necessary changes? As an old dog can you learn new tricks?

You can be assured that preparing for great performances is nobler in the mind, where time can stand still and practice can be endless and that…

If To Be Is Not To Be – Is That the Question?

While you ponder that question, here are some quotes to remind you of the importance and extent of well organised and meaningful mental prep…

- *"90% of the game is half mental."* **Yogi Berra**
- *"Competition is won or lost on the 6 inch playing field between the ears."* **Bobby Jones**
- *"Competitive toughness is an acquired skill and not an inherited gift."* **Chris Evert**
- *"The ability to conquer oneself is no doubt the most precious of all things sport bestows on us."* **Olga Korbut**
- *"I'm a firm believer in goal setting. Step by step. I can't see any other way of accomplishing anything."* **Michael Jordan**
- *"Obstacles are what you see when you take your eyes off your goal."* **Jim Lefebvre**
- *"The biggest thing is to have a mindset and a belief you can win every tournament going in."* **Tiger Woods**
- *"We all choke. Winners know how to handle choking better than losers."* **John McEnroe**
- *"Each point I play is in the now moment. The last point means nothing. The next point means nothing."* **Billie Jean King**
- *"The less tension and effort, the faster and more powerful you will be."* **Bruce Lee**

"If human beings did not have a tendency to interfere with their own ability to perform and learn, there would be no Inner Game. Similarly, if golfers hit every shot as well as they did their best ones, there would be no Inner Game of Golf. But the fact is that because of self-interference, few of us perform up to the level of our potential for more than brief moments at a time. Learning to get out of one's way is the purpose of the Inner Game."

Tim Gallwey –- Preface to The Inner Game of Golf

Finally…

"If I had six hours to chop down a tree, I would spend the first four hours sharpening the axe." **Abraham Lincoln**

PART 1 – What's in Your Basic Toolkit?

- Noticing the Senses
- Communication and Language – Verbal and Non-Verbal
- Rapport, Pacing and Leading
- Advanced Language Patterns
- Understanding States
- The Breathing Apparatus
- The R.A.S
- Sharpen up those Tools! – Practical Exercises

PART 2 – Using the Tools

- Voice
- Body Language
- Asking the Right Questions
- Sensory Acuity
- Visualisation
- State Breakers

PART 3 – Fitting the Appliances

A Catalogue for Re-Programming

> **Anchoring**
>
> **Collapsing Anchors**
>
> **Reframing**
>
> **Swish Pattern**
>
> **Circle of Excellence**
>
> **Timelining and Future Pacing**

Conventions in this book:

* = reference to a particular term or strategy in NLP and shown at the foot of the page. Within the subject there are many words and phrases that may be unfamiliar, so they are marked in *italics** with a full definition at the foot of the page

\# = Quotes and References are marked # and are listed at the foot of each page.

EXERCISES

Amongst the explanations in the book are many exercises, activities, games that you can do to sharpen up the tools, practice techniques etc. These can be identified by indented text headed by a

⇒

INTRODUCTION

Every scenario or paradigm and situation should have a goal or a collection of goals, outcomes that are worked towards. Without goals everything is *a propos* of nothing (as with *Dirk and Deke*…or maybe *All I Wanna Do* by Sheryl Crow).

The outcomes should be well-formed outcomes. The goals, whether arrived at by discussions about strategy or mutual consensus, should be tested to see whether they are SMART. Remember of course that big goals sometimes need to be broken down to a lot of smaller goals, and that these too should be well-formed and SMART. To find out what is meant by SMART Goals and well-formed outcomes look up page 99 towards the end of the book.

NLP and the ART of PLUMBING

I have set out to draw the analogy with you being like a plumber (or indeed any tradesman or mechanic). You have a basic NLP toolkit which you carry around with you at all times. In your everyday communication and interaction with your self and those around you, you may encounter anything from a "dripping tap" to a "collapsed drain" in amongst the smooth running waters. Your basic toolkit contains everything you need to find out how to best improve and enhance the situation. It will also give you the means of knowing which materials to go and get from the plumbers merchants to help you finish the job, so we can all wash our hands without getting our feet wet.

BASIC TOOLKIT

A good proportion of this is made up of what I would describe as your own *INNATE* skills. These comprise COMMUNICATION SKILLS and OBSERVATION SKILLS. We all have these to a greater or lesser degree and your knowledge, understanding and use of these skills can be practised and enhanced. You can become a better communicator and a better observer. This is the essence of much of the content of Part 1. As you read on you begin to understand more about *rapport** and how you can influence and persuade people towards areas that might be more beneficial to them

---

*Rapport: A relationship of responsiveness to self or others

There was a song some years ago entitled *"The Pina Colada song",* a big hit for Rupert Holmes. The lyrics were a story about a guy whose relationship was just meandering along and one night he read a small ad which caught his eye.
"If you like Pina Coladas and getting caught in the rain, etc …then I'm the love that you've looked for. Write to me and escape."
He followed it up because it was obviously written by someone who talked his language, sounded really interesting, shared his map. This person sounded much more interesting than his long-term partner! He arranges to meet this person and finds to his amazement that it is in fact his partner who put the entry in the small ads, because she was looking for someone more interesting as well. It's a story about rapport and what draws us to certain people. The more you understand about rapport, *pacing** and *leading**, the more you will reap the benefit.

Another vital tool in the kitbag covered in Part 1 is your state, states of mind, emotional states and how to control them better by re-mapping them. Starting with yourself, and then eventually how you can help, educate and guide your colleagues, players, teams or clients in the same positive way.

My old website blog has a page on breathing called *"Breath - The Stuff of Life."*
https://haveamindto.wordpress.com/2017/03/29/breath-the-stuff-of-life/

In making sure you get a good breathing apparatus for the toolkit I explain and outline how good breathing control will change your life. Not just purely in terms of health, but also for the doors it opens to state management, effective *visualization**, helping to build rapport and *pacing* and *leading*.

The R.A.S

The final topic in Part 1 is the *RAS** (see p49). The *RAS* is your brain's perceptive filter which (thankfully) reduces the millions of impulses bombarding us per second down to around 130 per second. In a conscious way, this fascinating tool is used sparingly, if at all, by most people in areas where peak performance counts. The *RAS* is hugely influential in the drawing and content of your maps, and you can begin to understand how it relates and adds to the effectiveness of your state management.

---

*Pacing: A matching or mirroring of another's behaviour
*Leading: Changing your own behaviour with rapport so others can follow
*Visualisation: The process of seeing images in your mind
*RAS: Reticular Activating System -The brain's perceptive filter

REALITY versus SUBJECTIVE EXPERIENCE

Another essential area to explore and to bear in mind in terms of communication is an understanding the balance between reality and subjective experience. What is reality after all? Which reality is more true, yours or mine? His, hers or theirs? If a tree falls in a forest and there is no one there to hear it, has it made a sound? Is the tree even there? What has led to you, me or them forming our various preferences in music or art; particular fragrances or colours; tastes and types of food?

Every one of the 5 senses brings with it interpretations of whatever reality we might wish to form. Part of human development of thought has been this realization: that we see, hear, feel, taste or smell is not irrefutably the truth/reality. The camera never lies … or does it? Sometimes even with the benefit of slow motion, people can still judge visual realities differently. You may have seen the demonstration of the notice containing this phrase or something very much like it:

> *"Finished files are the result of many years of careful scientific research and of undeniable proof".*

I have shown it to many groups, children and adults, over the years and then asked them how many "Fs" there are. It is an interesting example of the internal auditory processing and they are always surprised at how many different realities people have over just this little statement. (*The answer is 8.*)

Then there are the many philosophies, perspectives of the meaning of life, the universe, experience, language and interpretation. I think therefore I am. The brilliance of the answer to a philosophy exam question: "Is this a question?" where the student wrote "Well, if this is a question then this is an answer."

Take deductive logic for instance, which applies its reasoning from the general to the particular:

I was once sat listening to Prokofiev's Classical Symphony. My cousin came into the room and after listening for a bit said, "This is nice, what is it?" When I told her she replied, "Oh I don't like Prokofiev" and immediately walked out. Clearly, she had a positive feeling toward the music, but her negative image of the composer formed her eventual negative reaction.

Or this story from **Plato and a Platypus Walk into a Bar** #

An old cowboy goes into a bar and orders a drink. As he sits there sipping his whiskey, a young lady sits down next to him. She turns to the cowboy and asks him, "Are you a real cowboy?" He replies, "Well I've spent my whole life on the ranch, herding horses, mending fences and branding cattle, so I guess I am." She says, "I'm a lesbian. I spend my whole day thinking about women. As soon as I get up in the morning, I think about women. When I shower, or watch TV, everything seems to make me think of women." A little while later, a couple sits down next to the old cowboy and asks him, "Are you a real cowboy?" He replies, "I always thought I was – but I just found out I'm a lesbian."

Amusing as this is, it is worth noting that in addition to the subconscious mind not only dealing with positives it also deals in many ways, through deductive logic.

\# **Plato and a Platypus Walk into a Bar**
    by *Thomas Cathcart and Daniel Klein*

SPANNERS DON'T TIGHTEN SCREWS!

Part 2 covers how you use this basic toolkit.

This starts with your own voice, vocabulary and body language. These are vital to your success. Use them the right way and you'll "tighten the screws". Use them the wrong way and you might spend hours going around in circles wondering which route to take out of the maze. You might have the finest vocabulary in the world, but if the people can't hear you, or if you shout at them, the result will be the same. If you use beautiful language with a group of ten-year-olds, don't expect them to understand the content. Likewise, if you talk for half a minute in a monotone in any gathering, you will lose their attention.

You might have some speech impediment(s) or a particularly noticeable pitch of voice. These aren't such difficulties as you might

first think. If you study showbiz personalities who have these, you can see how they have used them to their advantage. Their confident and outgoing body language and *style of delivery* have totally masked their impediments.

GET A GOOD DELIVERY VEHICLE

Coaches and presenters know that anyway. Detailed explanation of points and running group sessions needs knowledge and, more importantly, clarity of delivery. So, knowledge of how to gain good rapport also needs a good delivery vehicle; your use of vocabulary, your voice and body language. And you have to be totally committed to driving that vehicle as well. You have to be like an actor, delivering a script in a convincing way with a view to achieving an excellent overall performance.

SENSORY ACUITY

Get attuned to reading people. They will give you all the information you need, some sooner than others. Read their body language. Listen to the words they use and the way they speak. Study their positions, hands, gestures, faces and eye-movements as they converse and communicate, and especially as they search internally for answers to questions.

THE ANSWER'S YES, NOW WHAT'S THE QUESTION?

The questions you ask are of key importance. They should be designed to break down barriers and provide information to you. You can use this information to help understand people even more. In plumbing terms, you need to know which room the dripping tap is in, before you need to know how fast it is dripping, and you don't really need to know how long it has been dripping, or what caused it to drip in the first place. Your next question would be to discover where the stop-cock is so you can turn the water off and mend the tap.

NLP models are quite simple in that regard. This question and answer routine is a great opportunity for dialogue, building rapport and giving you some bonuses for further helping your players, clients, teams and yourself.

GO AND GET THE APPLIANCE

Part 3 is your visit to the plumbers' merchant. Whether you need a washer for that tap, or a new boiler, this is the final piece of the jigsaw; getting and fitting the new device! There are many appliances for you to choose and some will work better than others. Some are remedies or renewals, like the ***reframing**** or ***swish pattern****, and some are creative and pro-active.

The secret here is your approach, and to know the result you want to achieve. In going from B to Q there are quite a few roads, routes to get there. The outcome is the desire. The process is the means. Find the optimal process to use and be flexible in your attitude. Don't go and get a new shower when a kitchen sink would be better. Washing dishes in the shower will work, but is not as effective. But that's how it is if you don't consider all the options.
"Swish pattern – that's what they need, and I like it, I'm good at it."
No! It might not be.

Don't be a slave to the appliance or to the road map. Look at Satellite Navigation for example. Brilliant concept, but practically and locally on the ground can be prone to huge flaws, as I found once visiting my uncle's farm in the dark. Instead of the drive to the farmhouse, I drove into a cornfield!

All actions in life are best done from a position of experience. What happened the first time you rode a bike? Being convincing comes from an inner assurance that the maps and strategies work for you. The best lead in to Part 3 is to look at the things YOU need in your life, whether it be personal or professional.

---

*Reframing: Understanding an experience in a different way, giving it a different meaning

*Swish Pattern: A process that programmes your brain to go in a new direction

Set about getting them sorted by choosing and working with the variety of appliances on offer. Once you see how things work and you get familiar with them, start using them and start gaining experience.

When working with NLP appliances I suggest you build up some experience of reframes as a starting point, because (a) there are many examples within the senses and (b) it is a comfortable way to "ease into the waters of this vast pool". You might then move on to look at *anchors** and *anchoring** as your next port of call. *Anchors* and reframes are the building blocks, the nuts and bolts, of all the appliances.

EXPERIENCE all the Dimensions

Everything I am pointing you towards is better learned from experience. Seeing, hearing and feeling the difference will be a really interesting experience for both for you and your colleagues, clients or players. Try the practicals and work the exercises. Widen and deepen your knowledge, broaden your competence and heighten your acuity.

The secret is..........getting things going by just **doing it**.

---

*Anchors: Triggers - visual, auditory or kinaesthetic - that link with an action or emotional state

*Anchoring: The process of associating one thing with another

PART 1 – Your Toolkit

NOTICING THE SENSES

There are five main ones, three of which are predominant. They are:

V   –   **Visual (what we see)**

A   –   **Auditory (what we hear)**

K   –   **Kinaesthetic (what we feel or touch)**

O   –   **Olfactory (what we smell)**

G   –   **Gustatory (what we taste)**

Everything we experience can be labelled as being in one of these five categories. The first three are primaries and for everyone there is usually one particular "preferred" or leading primary that forms the basis of the way we process our experience, the way we perceive our world (e.g. Can you see what I mean? Can you hear what I say? Do you feel ok with this?). This leading representational system is the way in which we literally represent our world, our experience, firstly to ourselves and then everyone else.

COMMUNICATION

Having begun to notice the senses, your own and other people's, continue to notice their orientation and their preferred representational system. Listen to their verbal communication, the particular words they use (as a preference) and you will start to get a fuller picture of what they are in terms of **V-A-K**. Take a moment of time to think...what is YOUR preferred system? Not sure?   **Take the quiz (p. 93)**

In terms of your toolkit, be aware that if you are a **K**inaesthetic person then when you talk to an **A**uditory person there will be something lost between you in their translation of your communication. Get on their wavelength (i.e. use their language system) and the level of communication between you will have much more mutual clarity. When talking to a group, get into the habit of talking in all three primary systems. That way you'll get your point(s) across to everyone without that process barrier. You will be hearing later when I get more to grips with the subject, how easy it is to see that this is a great help when cultivating rapport.

So that's verbal communication, but there's a vast amount of non-verbal communication by comparison. Over 90% of communication is non-verbal, a point well worth noting.

CALIBRATION

Calibration is what we need when reading with accuracy another person's body language or non-verbal signals. Like all our intuitive skills though, we can improve them by upgrading our qualities from seeing and noticing towards being an **observer**. The more you concentrate and focus on someone the more you can observe. That doesn't mean you have to stare at them so hard that they feel they are under a microscope, rather you have to open and widen your senses so you can gather more information. Pay more attention subtly and sensitively.

"I never really noticed that about them before..." you might hear someone say, which really sums up this point quite well. Noticing, however, is a sort of halfway house; it means "I think I know this person but here is a

feature, behaviour or action new to me". Now I've spotted it I might see it again and again.

⇒   *Another good practice exercise is to take a closer* **LOOK** *at the people being interviewed on TV. Read their non-verbal language as there's always plenty on view. Practice building up a picture of them in terms of their non-verbal language.*

So where am I taking you with this? You need to be a calibrator (an observer, not a notice-er or a see-er) and you need to be a conscious listener (not just a hearer or a listener-for). When you are at this level, these tools in your bag are at their sharpest and will serve you well.

They come in the section marked **PAYING ATTENTION**.

***Calibration:** Accurately recognising another person's state by reading non-verbal signals

LANGUAGE

As a communicator you need a good command of language. As a communicator in NLP you need a wider and fuller command of language. You need to be able to talk in many *sub-modalities**, especially in **V-A-K** language. You need to be able to express the same thing in many different ways. It's about broadening your vocabulary but in a different dimension.

⇒   *Think about key words you use a lot at work or in terms of coaching, managing or performance and make a vertical list. Now expand that list sideways with other words that have the same meaning. Along the way you'll probably start adding to the vertical list anyway ... and in the end you will run out of paper! It's a great exercise though and stimulates your thinking in ways you might not have even considered. The end result of course is a fuller experience for you – and for those you communicate with.*

Sometimes I use words when communicating with children that I know they won't understand, just to observe their reaction. Sometimes I give them two words together, one a lot simpler than the other. I have to read their body language as they don't always ask, *"what is that, what does that mean?"* As I'm practicing my calibration skills, I'm also helping them towards a fuller experience of language. Free yourself up and do the same. It's all part of being that "actor" or "performer". Everything should be a learning experience, whether for audience, yourself or, more likely, both.

---

*Sub-modalities: The special sensory qualities perceived by each of the senses

⇒ *How can you build your vocabulary? One way is the example above. It might only take you a few minutes. Get yourself a thesaurus or use an on-line one to help you. Another good way is to set yourself a daily goal of discovering two or three new words. A dictionary (or thesaurus) would be useful here also. If you keep it up, and start using the words regularly as well, then in a year you'll add over 1000 words to your vocabulary. It's a very easy habit to get into.*

Instructional commands

You need to expand your range of instructional commands so that they fit to what you are doing. Not everything can be achieved by using a series of barked *do this, don't do that orders*. In fact *don't do's* are to be avoided at all costs for this specific reason…

THE HUMAN BRAIN DOES <u>NOT</u> PROCESS DELETIVES

If I say **don't think of a black cat**, you have to first think of a black cat in order that you can try and carry out the instruction. So for a rugby player, "*I mustn't miss this kick*" will lead to a miss most likely, as the poor player's internal dialogue keeps trying to process missing the kick, the consequences of missing the kick, highlighting all the negatives on his MAP of his own kicking process.

Negative instructions bear a particularly bitter fruit when the stakes are raised. Playing a wrong note or missing a kick in practice is no big deal after all. But the same process in context on stage or in a packed stadium in a World Cup, would add an entirely different set of pressure variables.

They placed a piece of gymnastic apparatus, the beam, on the floor and invited a group to walk along it. At four inches wide it posed no internal or external problems, no physical or mental difficulties. The same beam was then suspended between two tall step ladders and the group was invited to walk along it. Reluctance spread like wildfire as the consequences were significantly raised. Falling off was now an issue as there was a prospect of pain and injury. If that group had been taught to walk blindfold perfectly along the beam would height have been an issue?

Many performance shortcomings can be laid at the feet of our internal dialogue, where our thoughts and words echo round the chart-room walls.

Invitational commands

As you use invitational commands, with an instruction to notice something and feedback information, you'll notice there's an immediate acceptance to carry out the task. And by also showing that the observational instruction is related to self-feedback, then it too is accepted as being of intrinsic value, and has an important personal element, self-worth. The best way we learn to perform tasks is through **personal experience**, especially an enjoyable and meaningful one, so design your instructions and strategies to focus on that experience as it will propel you and others to the next level using self-feedback. In NLP terms this conforms somewhat to the *TOTE Model**. (This is where you have a strategy, you run the strategy, and you adjust the strategy using feedback to improve it and re-run in a continuous loop until you are satisfied).

---

*The TOTE Model: All our outward behaviour is a result of these neurological processing patterns. Test - Operate - Test - Exit

Emphasis in delivery:

Think of the statement "I am going to the cinema". Now repeat it six times putting emphasis on each word in turn.

- *I* am going to the cinema
- I *am* going to the cinema
- I am *going* to the cinema
- I am going *to* the cinema
- I am going to *the* cinema
- I am going to the *cinema*

Six different meanings, yes? Emphasis points to words in a number of ways. Just as a magician might direct your attention away from the card he's just put up his sleeve, emphasis can be used to sneak covert commands past the conscious mind through the unconscious "back door". This is part of what is colloquially known as 'sleight of mouth'.

> ⇒ *A good exercise is to take a closer LISTEN to people in TV interviews (having already invited you to closely observe). Judge for yourself how articulate they are, and count up the number of "you knows" used (in particular in sports interviews). People for whom English is not their native language seem to use the phrase far less.*

Remember, articulation does not equate to intelligence but most people fall into the trap and think this is so. It is really all about usage and practice.

Language (verbal and non-verbal) is the "Swiss Army Knife" of tools in your toolkit. It can pick the lock of even the largest, heaviest doors.

A lady came to me with an addiction to fizzy drinks. Her sugar intake was destroying all attempts at dietary control. Various other methods of control and different advisors had failed for her. I pointed out that her weekly spend, which was vast, was equivalent to her being a major shareholder in "Coca Cola Ltd".

I merely suggested she start investing the same amount in "Herself Ltd" instead, something others had never suggested to her.

She remarked: "I'd never looked at it in those terms before"

Just this small reframe did the business for her in conquering the compulsions. Never be too surprised at the speed at which things can change. Even casual remarks can be catalysts to large personal changes and amendments to behaviour.

RAPPORT

Rapport is a relationship, a dialogue, a sort of dance. It's a relationship of mutual respect and influence, and comes from an honest attempt to see the world from the other person's point of view. For the dance to be an aesthetic pleasure both partners must be in step with each other. For the dialogue to work, each party must be able to express themselves, as well as sympathetically listening to the other.

If you study people in rapport, especially in a social context, they are matched in both their verbal and non-verbal communication. The nuances of their behaviour and language are also matched.

Non-verbal matching can be seen via general posture, speed of movements, speed and loudness of speech, rate and depth of breathing and eye contact.

Verbal matching was mentioned in earlier chapters, when using language particular to certain representational systems or using different words but of a similar meaning. This also leads on to *matched* thinking.

You can be in rapport with people you don't necessarily like, so long as there is mutual respect there. However, most of us are drawn towards people who are like ourselves, because essentially we understand and empathise with them more. We speak each other's language verbally and non-verbally, we see the world in the same way and as such we are compatible and congruent.

So, in your basic toolkit is rapport and you need to be aware of how to build it and use it so you are a more effective communicator. Whilst it is more straightforward to cultivate rapport with an individual, how do you go about it with an audience or a group?

"He had the audience eating out of his hand…" is a well-known phrase … but it gives a clue to what is happening. They were eating (so they were doing something) and it was out of his hand – so there was a connection, a dialogue, a dance. He was leading them in the dance. But it had to have started somewhere! And it was about engaging them, relaxing them and getting their attention. Good comedians are in rapport with their audience and it is built by planning a routine. You need to plan your routine, however basic, so you can get the dance going.

You need to engage them so, for me, eye contact is vital. If you are looking over their heads, or talking to an imaginary person at the back of the room, then they (individually and collectively) will read your body language accordingly. And that says what? I'm talking at you not to you or with you; I'm either nervous or consider myself superior to you; am I really interested in either you OR what I've got to say? There could be a number of other things thrown in there as well, but I've written enough reasons to cut to the very heart of rapport.

Respect your group or audience; relax them and put them at their ease; if you know some of them, use their names. People love being addressed directly as they feel important and valued – if you don't know them find out their names as this will let them know you are interested in them. Read their language and you'll know if you are getting their attention well enough to take the next step; talk in all three representational systems (**V-A-K**); ask them questions if possible.

This will all sound very basic and obvious and it comes with practice, but building rapport makes all communication so much more enjoyable, easier and meaningful for you, your players and clients, and for your team. With individuals it is a simpler, somewhat different dance, but the key elements are there just the same:

Mutual respect → Rapport → Trust

Be relaxed. Observing and listening is much easier if <u>you</u> are at ease. Talk in an engaging way, look for areas where you can match their movements and other body language, match their verbal language and at the same time discover their representational system. **Be respectful.** Remember *matching* is not *copying* or *mimicking*. This will lose it for you at a stroke. Be subtle and be natural. It's probably best to practise matching in social rather than working contexts.

All these behavioural skills I am encouraging you to hone, to work on, you will not be able to improve or master at once. It will take time and practice which you can do by advancing in little chunks – and this is why, almost daily, you can formulate a little plan (in advance) of what you want to achieve in terms of improvement. If you have a desire, a goal to work towards, you will get there much quicker and with more pleasure along the way if you are organised and have a plan.

PACING and LEADING

Pacing and leading I have already alluded to when talking about rapport. It is very much the way you might use rapport to guide the people you are communicating with into a different state. Using the dance analogy, you might start off as matching your partner's steps (*paces*) rather as they would be the dominant partner, and then you would by design, influence and rapport *lead* them to another place by becoming yourself the dominant partner.

It relies on rapport, that trust and mutual understanding and respect you have engendered, so you can subtly encourage (but not quite coax or seduce) them to another more mutually beneficial place.

Pacing and leading is one of the keys to influencing people. It refers to meeting them at their map of the world (pacing) and then taking them where you want them to go (leading).

It can be done in verbal and non-verbal ways but is most effective using a mixture of both. Non-verbal is quite straightforward, by using mirroring or matching and then by allowing your own behaviour to change, to develop, and to encourage the other people to follow your lead. Breathing is a good example here, because breathing in "sync" can be subtly changed by a leader talking and making his breathing pattern changes noticeable to others.

> ⇒ *Have you ever yawned whilst talking or in a group and noticed how soon after that other people have also yawned? Sometimes it is an almost instantaneous response. Similarly, you can look up and appear to be observing something with interest, and their eyes will soon follow and look into the same area. If you set out to do this with a goal, a purpose, you can move their distracted attention around almost at will.*

ADVANCED LANGUAGE PATTERNS

Please don't be put off here. We are talking patterns, not the language itself, and it is the subtlety of patterns that make this exercise even more interesting.

The particular language patterns I will highlight here are embedded commands and *presuppositions**, although the *etceteras* under this heading are profuse and these are sometimes described as subliminal or hypnotic language.

***Presuppositions:** Ideas or beliefs that are pre-supposed, taken for granted and acted upon

Take a look at this conversational extract from a possible coaching scenario…

> *"As you listen to what I have said about building this skill and you pay particular attention to each part of the exercise, you have thoughts, in your mind, about what I'm saying and how you can begin to incorporate this material into your game. And as you have thoughts and have the feelings that you are having, you find that this is something that really interests and benefits you and because of that it will be easy for you to learn. And as you wonder about being able to understand and learn what I've said here, you begin to think about where in your game you can use this process and what outcome you might want to obtain by using this skill. And you wonder how you can set aside enough time to really learn these skills to improve your results"*

Hypnotic language such as this is quite noticeable since it often begins each sentence in this way: "As you are doing something," or: "And you may wonder," or: "And you may have thoughts."   (For wondering is to have thoughts and/or feelings after all.)   And so as you notice what is written above, you might start to ponder what sentences are pacing and which ones are leading. Here it is again with the *leaders* highlighted:

"As you listen to what I have said about building this skill and you pay particular attention to each part of the exercise, you have thoughts, in your mind, about what I'm saying and how **you can begin to incorporate this material into your game.** *And as you have thoughts and have the feelings that you are having,* **you find that this is something that really interests and benefits you and because of that it will be easy for you to learn.** *And as you wonder about being able to understand and learn what I've said here,* **you begin to think about where in your game you can use this process and what outcome you might want to obtain by using this skill. And you wonder how you can set aside enough time to really learn these skills to improve your results"*

There is a pattern here as well which seems to build towards a "leading" crescendo: P – P – P – L / P – P – L – L / P – L – L – L

So, having identified the pacing and leading elements let's just look at the extract from the point of view of embedded commands…

"As you **listen to what I have said about building this skill** *and you* **pay particular attention to each part of the exercise**, *you have thoughts, in your mind, about what I'm saying and how you can* **begin to incorporate this material into your game**. *And as you have thoughts and have the feelings that you are having, you* **find that this is something that really interests and benefits you** *and because of that* **it will be easy for you to learn**. *And as you wonder about being able to* **understand and learn what I've said here**, *you begin to* **think about where in your game you can use this process** *and what outcome you might want to obtain by using this skill.*

And you wonder how **you can set aside enough time to really learn these skills** *to improve your results..."*.

Are you beginning to see the bigger picture here and hear everything start to click into gear in perfect harmony? Intriguing, isn't it?

And as we take one more look at the extract for **pre-suppositions**...

"As you listen to what I have said about building this skill and you pay particular attention to each part of the exercise, **you have thoughts, in your mind, about what I'm saying** *and how* **you can begin to incorporate this material into your game"**.

The highlighted statements are pre-supposed since you are listening and paying attention to what I have said...

"...and as you have thoughts and have the feelings that you are having, **you find that this is something that really interests and benefits you** *and* **because of that it will be easy for you to learn.**

Because you have thoughts and feelings you find ... etc and therefore it will be easy to learn!

And as you wonder about being able to understand and learn what I've said here, **you begin to think about where in your game you can use this process** *and* **what outcome you might want to obtain by using this skill**. *And you wonder how* **you can** *set aside enough time to really learn these skills to* **improve your results"**

You may perhaps be wondering how some of these elements overlap and, that being so, will their effect be altered in some way? The joy of using advanced language patterns is precisely this flexibility and it is worth knowing and being reassured that everything here is getting in under the radar. Plus, by using subtle emphasis and voice tones the whole nature of what is being said can be covertly overlaid even more.

And the outcome is quite different from what might have seemed at first. Talking this way does take practice, and as you do it bit by bit, day by day, you find it becomes unconscious competence as does all regular practice. You can become increasingly confident that every single bit of what you say to people is having an effect. Leave no stone unturned, leave no tone unstirred, or (as someone once said about theatre critics) leave no turn un-stoned!

I've probably stimulated more than a few grey cells with the illustrations on this topic. Now you can understand why language is *SO* important in gaining rapport, pacing and leading.

UNDERSTANDING STATES

I've put understanding states into the basic toolkit because it is essential to what you are and how you are, essential to your team and/or clients and what and how they are and essential to your mutual interaction.

Understanding and controlling your own state is fundamental to your everyday life. If you have both understanding and control, your life is enriched, purposeful and rewarding. Without it you are at the mercy of your emotions and of every event that your path crosses and that crosses your path and of those where there is the occasional collision. This recipe is fraught with problems and can sometimes be a living hell.

A distorted map? Every lemming has one. The irony is that most people (and all lemmings) fall into the latter "at the mercy of" category. In **Unlimited Power** #, Tony Robbins describes it along these lines:

> *"...Have you ever had the experience of being on a roll, feeling that you could do no wrong? A time when everything seemed to go right? Where every shot or move in the match went easily and perfectly – an exam or meeting where you had all the answers? Maybe it was a time when you amazed yourself by doing something heroic or dramatic you never thought you could do. You've probably had the opposite experience too; A day when nothing went right. Everything you did messed up, every step was wrong, every door was locked, everything you tried turned out wrong. What's the difference? You're the same person. You should have the same resources at your disposal.*
>
> ***The difference is the neurophysiological state you are in.***
>
> *There are enabling states: confidence, love, inner strength, joy, ecstasy, belief, that tap great wellsprings of personal power. There*

are paralyzing states: confusion, depression, fear, anxiety, sadness, frustration, that leave us powerless.
We all go in and out of good and bad states. The difference is being pro-active or re-active".

We get up in the morning in a particular state (or mood) and our day and all we experience is coloured by that state. The weather, contents of our mail, the atmosphere at work, the people we meet, maybe our training or practice later ALL interact with our state; amplifying or diminishing it by degrees. If we are, however, reactive to all that happens to us, "I'm having a bad day" is often our opinion if it's going to pieces, and this merely serves as negative and amplifying feedback.

Try to remember a day when things went badly for you. Remember how you felt and how you reacted to events. You probably feel uncomfortable just recalling what happened, as you represent it to yourself. Now imagine objectively what that day would have been like if you had **controlled** your disposition and reacted differently to events. Does the emotional discomfort diminish as you plot the daily course with a different map?

So, the events, the weather, the people; everything that impinged upon your life that day would have been the same. It was your reaction that was different. Your positive state prevailed and your view of life was much better as a result.

Unlimited Power, *Tony Robbins*

The focus of this argument and example is…that when you are seeking to **control the controllables**, the greatest controllable is YOU and your STATE. By allowing yourself to be a victim of your emotions (and we are all prone to doing this in varying degrees) you are no longer in control.

Control here is not the kind as (say) viewed by the control-freak who compulsively wants to impose their map onto everybody. Control is awareness and direction of your thoughts and the way you process your own feelings. **Positive/Neutral/Negative**. You can choose

As Tony Robbins further describes it in terms of personal power #

"….You start every day with 100%. Every time you process or experience an event, in terms of personal emotion that bank of power gets drawn upon. Every time you react emotionally and hand some personal control away it depletes that power bank".

Stubbing your toe; spilling your coffee; a large bill in the mail; idiot driver on the road; bad tempered boss at work etc. These events can build up through the day compounded by your negative reactions until later on you meet your partner and dump all your bad reaction onto them. They might do the same back to you having had their own bad day. Now your relationship is on a collision course! Arguments ensue, and so the whole cycle goes on, feeding into the next day … stress, anxiety, negativity, depression … where will it end?

This spiral of events was in your hands right from the start of the day. Accidents are accidents. Be objective and move on. A bill is just a piece of paper, not a dagger in the heart. View it in the context of the big picture, be financially objective. It isn't a personal attack on your lifestyle. The idiot driver isn't that. Like Korzybski's Joe, he's just committed a minor incompetence. He hasn't personally set out to attack YOU. Remember your emotional reaction (maybe rage) is also an incompetence, with a lot more potential danger. The roads don't need another agitated, unfocussed, enraged, emotionally charged driver on them. Bad tempered boss? His problem, not yours. Don't let his problem spill over to become your problem. Laugh or smile at him, help him, **pace and then lead** him to a calmer place. Engage, don't react.

By now, if you have been saying, "Yes that's all well and good BUT I can't do that," then you probably find the reserves in your power bank run dry on quite a regular basis. The YES-BUT answer usually means, "I know my map is faulty but I can't change it". Try this solution: Take the scenes of events and detach yourself from them. Make them into an old black white film that you are watching of yourself on a small cinema screen. Now how does it feel? If it is still bad, take yourself up into the projection room in that cinema. Now look down at you in the cinema seat watching you in the film on the screen, and run the film again. Feel different? Run the film slower/faster/backwards. Feeling different now?

What I'm doing here is getting you to **REFRAME** your experience, to pull the plug on this bad day and to illustrate how easy it is to detach from the emotion of your reaction to events. This way you can be more objective and start to build your own state control. The more you do it, the better you become. It's like any competence … and let's face it, you are pretty competent at being a victim of your emotional reactions!

Now we've mopped that up, you can appreciate why I've put state control into the toolkit.

So, you have someone (perhaps it is you) who beats themselves up when they try a routine and gets it wrong. How can you best help them? They need to control their state before they have any remote chance of building competence in the skill you might be working on. PLUS, they'll be doing this for everything they do, every time anything goes wrong (even slightly wrong). Some days will be worse than others but they're clearly a victim of their emotions. They're most likely a perfectionist, working with a map that allows no scope for trial and error. Remind them there is no failure, only feedback.

Take a moment to consider how ever do crawling babies get to be toddlers. If there was no internal learning feedback (**The TOTE Model**) and no external encouragement then the process would be much lengthier. Fortunately, all babies' learning is by experiential feedback. If this was not the case then their metamorphosis of motion would be via an external (someone else's) map. Pity the baby with ludicrously perfectionist parents as they observe their child's repeated attempts to stand up and walk. Their maps accept no failures, no errors and so as they watch baby repeatedly falling over they say, "Oh dear, what a shame. I guess little Joe won't be a walker."

I often refer to a character known as the *"Beat-Up Kid"*… and you'll recognise him. This guy is not his own best friend. His map is built on perfection, not just in performance but in practice. He won't allow himself to make mistakes without castigating and criticizing and lots of people have this in varying degrees. It's a map that is built up through their childhood, often the intense desire to do well for external approval rather than intrinsic pleasure. This is formed because their pleasure is derived from that external approval more than for their inner selves.

Helping the Beat-Up Kid

Use your skills of rapport, pacing and leading. It's not a lengthy process. If engagement is harder to initiate (if his mental bath is overflowing) then you need to use a state breaker, something that will distract him for long enough so you can get into his mental bathroom, pull the plug out and turn off the taps. Talk, empathise, ask questions, start enacting solutions and he'll soon notice that you care, you're concerned, you *want* to help, you *can* help and you *are* helping.

The Beat-Up Kid is usually full of negative self-talk, so the clue is that there's a carping, critical, damning voice in there somewhere, speaking harshly, judgementally. He's an **A**uditory person. And there is perhaps your solution for him also. **REFRAME the voice**.

The states you encounter might not necessarily be negatively emotionally charged either. You will encounter flaccid, disinterested and washed out states too. There'll also be lack of focus or concentration or lack of motivation perhaps. Be prepared for these and consider what might work to break state or lead here. Gaining rapport too could be a real challenge. You will be faced with it at some stage or maybe you've already come into contact with it and have thrown in your own towel or just walked away. Consider the solutions you might have now, as you are aware of your new interests, competences and are building super-charged inter-personal communication skills.

THE BREATHING APPARATUS

There MUST be room in your basic toolkit for your breathing apparatus. Everything about performance, preparation for performance and regular interaction revolves around proper breathing, an understanding of how and why it works and, if necessary, retraining of the pattern of this most vital of your autonomic processes is absolutely essential.

Abdominal Breathing:

If you study a baby's breathing pattern you will notice a rise and fall of the stomach area and chest but not in the shoulders. Now study your own breathing pattern in the same respect. Probably, something has changed along the way, as you have grown. Nobody taught the baby how to breathe, but certainly we, as we have grown up, have taken on various different patterns for a variety of reasons, mostly detrimental.

When I demonstrate *abdo* breathing to children I am always amazed to find that even by the ages of 9 and 10 they already take in what they think is a "deep breath" by moving their shoulders upwards to initiate and drive the process rather than using the diaphragm. When I show them the correct way they usually laugh at first as my belly expands, but as they do it for a short while they discover how much better they feel. And they also notice that their recovery from exertion using deep *abdo* breathing happens much quicker.

If I ask you to stand to attention, along with straightening your back and stiffening up, part of your perceived "improvement of posture" will be to draw your stomach in and push your chest out. In THIS position however, the diaphragm functions far less well and you are forced to breathe in a shallow way by expanding the upper chest. In stressful states we are prone to shallow breathing, a pattern which merely fills the top of the lungs. Abdominal breathing fills the lungs up from the bottom upwards. This results in a greater intake of oxygen, with obvious positive consequences. It is not just that oxygen is the brain's main fuel either. The calming, almost therapeutic effect of filling the lungs thus and exhaling slowly is well documented.

> ⇒ So, abdo breathing is very beneficial, and it is vital to practise the technique until it is second nature. You can start out by 1 minute at a time sequences. Place your hand on your navel and breathe in at the bottom of your lungs (for a count of 5), feeling your hand being pushed outwards on the inhale. Hold for a count of 3, then exhale for a count of 7, feeling your hand move inwards. This way you will get a 4-5 breaths per minute cycle. As you perform the cycle really concentrate on the process and nothing else. You will notice a calming effect and a feeling of detachment, all in addition to a fulfilling intake of oxygen. Do this as many times in the course of the day as you can remember. Remembering the "law of 21", it is likely that after this lapse of time abdo breathing will be assimilated into and become your normal breathing pattern.

THE R.A.S

Before your eyes glaze over as you murmur the word *jargon* let me touch on a bit of the scientific here. The R.A.S or Reticular Activating System is the brain's perceptive filter. If this filtering did not take place then we would go into conscious information overload, as much of the sensual information is repetitive or less relevant.

Ever made a sound recording in a classroom or at a party? There is just so much background noise picked up that you would wonder how on earth people can hold conversations with that entire extraneous din.

You live in a town, with lit streets at night and then go for a holiday in the country or where the streets aren't lit. How dark is it at night? Unnerving almost, and likewise for the country dweller trying to sleep in a city-based hotel. Too bright, noisy streets…the examples go on…

The RAS consists of a bundle of densely packed nerve cells located in the central core of the brainstem. Roughly the size of a little finger, the RAS runs from the top of the spinal cord into the middle of the brain. This area of tightly packed nerve fibres and cells contains nearly 70% of your brain's estimated 200 billion nerve cells or a total of 140 billion cells.

To get back to the noisy party scenario…in all the cacophony you may hear your name spoken by someone at the other side of the room. Your RAS has picked it up as relevant data and placed it in the "in-tray" of your consciousness.

The best thing about the RAS is its programmability. You can direct it in a whole variety of ways, and in a whole variety of directions. Your RAS is arguably the most powerful tool in your kit and now you have an awareness of it you can begin to understand its capabilities and have more and more creative thoughts about how you might use it.

PRACTICAL EXERCISES to SHARPEN UP THOSE TOOLS

NOTICING the SENSES – and focusing your R.A.S:

⇒ **Visual:** To make this practice even better wear some ear plugs. Choose a small common object. Place it a few feet away and now begin to study it closely, so closely that you can remember many different things about it. When you are ready, close your eyes and see how many things about that image you can now remember. How clear and detailed is the picture? Remember that and open your eyes and see how many points you missed. Study it again – with even more detailed scrutiny. Close your eyes again now, and see how much more information is in your visual memory. If you spend a few minutes each day on this visual sharpening exercise it will hone your perception.

⇒ **Auditory:** Sit quietly with your eyes closed or blindfolded and allow yourself to notice more about the sounds of things going on around you. If there is a clock ticking, then listen to the silences between the ticks. With the visual sense switched off you will realise, after about a minute, that your awareness and focus has shifted to auditory and there are suddenly many extra sounds that your perceptive filter (RAS) has been ignoring, sometimes in a quite random way.

⇒ **Kinaesthetic:** Sit quietly and shut off the V and A senses with blindfold and ear plugs. Now take another common object (or maybe even the same object) and allow your fingers to explore it. Notice as much as you can about it using your sense of touch. Notice the things your body comes in contact with; the seat you are in, your feet on the floor. Really focus on how everything feels. Allow your tongue to explore your mouth and your hands to explore your facial features.

⇒   There is a game you can play with friends. Each of you chooses an object for someone else to explore while blindfolded. See if they can identify it just by touch. This game can be extended to include smells and tastes. Also there are sometimes radio quizzes that ask people to identify certain recorded sounds.

Exercises that direct and focus the R.A.S:

⇒   These are really useful as well and I have already mentioned the one with the ticking clock where you focus on the silences. In recorded music, try and follow the line of one particular instrument. Try this visual RAS focus next time you are a passenger on a car journey. For a few minutes just focus and count up the number of red cars you see. At the end of that time try and remember how many white cars or lorries you saw. All you saw (or focused on) was red cars so your perception (your map) of the traffic content in that short period was vague but for red cars.

It has been said that if you put a pickpocket into a room full of saints then all he'll see is their pockets! Take this a stage further and you can see how a person who is depressed, or pessimistic, likes strong coffee or is attracted to blondes will have their RAS more perceptually focused in those directions. (Remember the cowboy?)

If you believe the world contains good, kind, caring and loving people then your RAS will filter in for you all sorts of experiences that go to back up those beliefs. If you believe that people are cynical, ungenerous, spiteful or indifferent then you won't have to look too hard to find experiences that reinforce those beliefs either. Plenty of examples of both abound.

Your RAS is the set of implements with which you draw your map of the world and the palette that colours it.

Know your lead re-presentational system? Take the quiz to help you find out.

COMMUNICATION

⇒ *The best exercises here are to be as observant as possible about other people. This is best practised socially at gatherings or even walking around town streets. Get used to not just seeing, watching and noticing but REALLY observing. Gathering as much information as you can.*

⇒ *An interesting 5–minute exercise in social contexts is to work as a group - each observing other people (in the room but outside the group) and saying what type of job you think they might have, or speaking voice or where they come from. See how the judgements differ within the group. Each of you discusses your reasons for whichever judgements you have made. In the end, nominate someone to go and find out the real answers.*

⇒ *This exercise can be adapted into a game for groups, where each person has a card with a working/personality/geographical type and they have to act out being that person. Here everyone else has to discover as much as they can about "you", based upon your portrayal.*

LANGUAGE

⇒ *For all the five senses in turn, make a list of as many sub-modalities as you can. How many different taste-related words can you list for instance? (Sweet, sharp, tart, acidic, luscious, cool, tangy, mouthwatering, bitter, spicy...)*

⇒ *For group work this could become a game situation. It's amazing how quickly you can expand your usage and vocabulary this way. Add some words to your lists every day, because every day and in every way you get better and better.*

PART 2 – Using the Tools

UNCONSCIOUS INCOMPETENCE →	CONSCIOUS INCOMPETENCE ⇩
UNCONSCIOUS COMPETENCE	CONSCIOUS COMPETENCE

⇦

The Learning Cycle

All the topics in Part 2 have already been mentioned, as I gave you the outline of all the items in the basic toolkit. How good, sharp or well-functioning those tools are is your responsibility. If you haven't got some of them yet then your task will be harder, but not impossible. Work through the exercises as these will help you move through the learning cycle from what is now perhaps conscious incompetence towards unconscious competence. The main thing is you now have an awareness of what's needed so you can deal with the overflowing bath, dripping tap, or even installing a new boiler.

Let's start at the very beginning, a very good place to start (rather than, say, the middle!)

Communication and language

VOICE

Essentially your voice needs dimensions. These are height and depth, tone or timbre, volume; these are the very basics. There are a huge number of descriptions of voice qualities which can be found here at the **National Centre for Voice and Speech** website:

http://www.ncvs.org/ncvs/tutorials/voiceprod/tutorial/quality.html

> ⇒ *At my first practical workshop, the course tutor did a simple demo which gave everyone an idea of how voice can be changed through various areas of the body. Using two fingers of your right hand press your nose as you say, "This is my nose," and so on down for mouth, throat, chest, abdomen. Note the changes. Try talking from these different places; try talking with different accents – notice how the breathing, mouth shape, and centre of delivery differs.*

Breathing Properly

As you improve your breathing, you will improve your voice qualities and the number of voices you can use with ease. For those of you who glossed over the section on the breathing apparatus then I implore you to go back and learn and install it.

My old website had a page on breathing which I have now posted on the Blog, "Mind How You Go", here:
https://haveamindto.wordpress.com/2017/03/29/breath-the-stuff-of-life/

It broadens the subject for you and also has links to Optimal-Breathing.com, arguably the most comprehensive website on proper breathing. Proper breathing is a pre-requisite for State Management and all the other physical and mental competences mentioned in this book.

Another essential your voice needs is **Clarity of Diction** as a basic. If you want to deliver vital words and phrases, whether it's for coaching, singing, a presentation or an *ad hoc* script for pacing and leading, then clarity should come as standard. If it doesn't, you'll lose the point, and very soon you'll lose your audience. You don't have to be a sergeant-major or a Shakespearean "actaw", but you do have to have a good delivery vehicle. If your plumber's van doesn't get you to the call-out how can you effect any changes?

To sum up, your voice has to be interesting. Some people have interesting and even beautiful voices and they could read the phone book to you and it would be an engaging pleasure.

> ⇒ Exercise:
> *Listen to people on TV and radio and judge their voices with these things in mind. What makes them a pleasure (or otherwise) to listen to, what qualities have they got over the next person? Make a list of some voices you know that are memorable for whatever reason and compare them all. Do they have qualities that you can model? We all admire the impressionists and if you get a chance, listen to them explaining how they practice their art and the things they look for as well as listen for.*

> ⇒ *Try being an impressionist yourself, or have a game as a group.*

BODY LANGUAGE

As I mentioned before, your body language is a crucial part of your delivery vehicle. Every movement you make (or don't make) should be essential to what you are doing. Even accidents like tripping over should/can be used as part of your delivery. It could be a perfect state breaker after all, not necessarily yours but for the player(s). Try doing one on purpose with a view to achieving some end such as an ice breaker or a state breaker. See what happens. You want them *eating out of your hand*, then put them at ease. If they see you laughing at yourself or at ease with that situation, then this will build rapport ... and allow you to pace and lead.

Eye contact is crucial. It is part of the dance, AND it will give you clues about your audience and their view of the world. You'll come across some who avoid it, but it need only be a fleeting glance which you WILL be able to get if you ask them to watch for something or give them something to hold while you keep talking about something else. Distraction is the usual key to animating someone who is very 'internal'.

> ⇒ *Exercise:*
> *Get them to examine their own body language. If working with a group, ask one or two to act the role of the Beat-Up Kid, and then get people to examine how to correct the behaviour and attitude in a positive way.*
>
> ⇒ *Charades is a great game for practising body language.*
>
> ⇒ *Watch silent movies and mime artists and try miming some scenes yourself.*

ASKING THE RIGHT QUESTIONS

Asking questions sets up a direction of thought in the mind and engages the unconscious to find answers. Asking the right kind of questions will set the mind along a path that enriches and enlivens to the point that often the answers are not as important as asking the question. So what questions can you ask that will make a huge difference for yourself or to your players?

This is a very meaty topic, but without wishing to put off some people out there, let me assure you that I will explain it as tastefully as I can. Questions are the main way you can explore issues for yourself and others and help them to be resolved. Look at these examples when discussing a particular goal:

If I achieve this goal, what will it get for me?
When I achieve this goal, what will it get for me?
When I achieve this goal, what will it mean for me?

Question 1 is to be avoided because of the IF. It is an assumption of doubt, and will be unconsciously interpreted as a lack of confidence by you about your (or their) ability to succeed. Question 3 is better but is going to elicit vague answers, because it might mean a range of things for you (or them) from values right through to associations and other outcomes. Question 2 is quite specific since it presupposes the goal will be achieved and will draw out specific answers. "Get" and "mean" bring out different results, if you get my meaning.

According to O'Connor and Lages#, powerful questions have 5 key characteristics.

- *They usually begin with the word "What".*
- *They lead to action.*
- *They are oriented towards goals rather than problems.*

- They lead the person into the future rather than dwell on the past.
- They contain powerful assumptions that are helpful for the person.

Questions that begin with "why" are enquiring and occasionally imply blame. So rather than say, *"Why did you think that happened?"* or, *"Why did you do that?"* it is better to say, *"What do you think caused that?"* or, *"What do you think happened as you did that?"*
Each question has the same desired answer, but with different wording you will get better answers, and better answers will make the next stage much more straightforward.

"What caused you to drop the ball?" is a far better question than *"Why did you drop the ball?"* But you might even jump a stage and ask, *"What do you need to do to catch the ball next time?"* especially as the embedded command is in there!

This question requires an answer involving some action X that needs to be taken, and the question is oriented <u>towards</u> the goal of catching the ball, not <u>away</u> from dropping the ball. The question also leads the player into the future especially as it contains the assumption that if you always do X then the ball will always be caught. In an individual or group context this form of question asking is positive and outcome driven. It implies that mistakes are learning situations and errors are essential to proper learning.

This is something very useful and powerful, if you think back to our friend the **"Beat-Up Kid"** for example.

Coaching with NLP, *Joseph O'Connor and Andrea Lages*

CHALLENGING QUESTIONS

Challenging questions are great for getting to the core of people's limiting beliefs. These limiting beliefs might take the form of over-generalisations or unconsidered opinions. For example, *"I'll never be any good at that,"* which you have already encountered and perhaps wondered how to best tackle.

> ⇒ *A lad of fifteen was referred to me for a one-to-one by his cricket manager. He was ostensibly a bowler but had said "I can't bat" which was clearly untrue and was starting to put the skids under his whole game. Whilst I did not pursue his original statement when I met him, let's assume it was me who had heard this original overgeneralization. The way into starting to help break that down would be to ask him "Is that always the case, or just some of the time?" and, "Who says that?" followed by, "What evidence do you have that backs that up?" Once I'd got answers to the first two (the "when" and "who"), then the "what" question will really start him on the road towards feeling better about his batting. Based upon the evidence he gave me, I now had his view of the world as it related to his cricket; his opinions and generalisations about his batting.*
>
> *After correcting a couple of physical shortcomings, I then asked what felt physically different now and how he might notice anything else about how he was now playing. His whole persona became much more upbeat and positive, and he couldn't wait to carry on shaking off the metaphorical cobwebs. As a bonus, he also opened up with his own view of what had led him to pass the judgement he had, and that how it was clear now that it was a thing of the past. He now has proof to himself that he can bat, and will no doubt move on to the next level. The bonus here was that*

by pointing him in a positive direction he was now able to give credence to his self-analysis, and thus put the former limitations to bed once and for all.

That example was from obvious over-generalisation and also unconsidered opinion. We all judge our capabilities in terms of past experience focused for us by our RAS. We go and read our various maps.

But many children in their early and mid-teens view this based not on last week, but last year when they were physically smaller, weaker, with a shorter visual and judgemental perspective. I like to mention to them that a lot of the work we are doing is preparing them for 1 or 2 years hence, when these skills and competences will really come into their own. They all want to feel grown-up…and this gives them a goal measured in the context of that feeling, and gives them perhaps the strongest motivation to practise and get better at it.

Look out for use of pressure words…words like **should** or **must** and their negative equivalents **shouldn't** or **mustn't**. Reframe their use with **can** and **will** or **can't** or **won't**. It puts an action or a purpose into the statement.

Challenge these uses as well. I **mustn't** miss this kick is (as already said) an absolute no-no, but it sounds quite different when it becomes I **won't** miss this kick. Challenging it with a *"What would happen if you do?"* might get you a pretty obvious answer I know. It leads on to an opportunity to ask, *"What do you need to do make that happen?"* You might even jump in with that question straightaway as a matter of urgency of course.

I'm certain now you have an idea about the nature and importance of the right questions. Questions provide answers so you can act accordingly.

⇒ *Make yourself a list of 3-5 things that you feel are holding you back or that you cannot improve upon. Write down for each what reasons you have for arriving at those judgements. Study your answers closely and see if you can formulate another set of questions (along the lines just discussed) that might give you a new perspective on those judgements. Keep asking yourself challenging questions until you have exposed your limiting beliefs and faced them head on.*

SENSORY ACUITY

Eye accessing cues

Looking at the other person

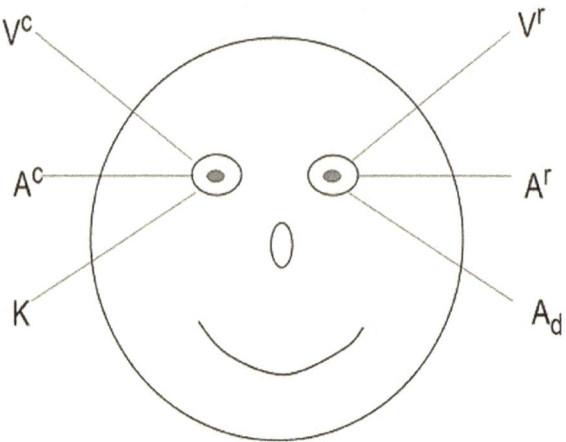

Get as familiar as possible with this activity and these positions.

⇒ *Practise this on friends and family – ask them a question about a remembered picture and their eyes should go to the **Vr** position (they go up left); ask them to imagine what something might look like (a constructed image not one in memory) and they should go to the **Vc** position (up right). Ask them to remember what something sounds like and they should go to the **Ar** position, and likewise to the opposite position for constructed sounds (**Ac**). Ask them to remember how something felt (physically or emotionally) and they should go to the **K** position. Down left is usually auditory digital (**Ad**). Auditory digital relates to internal dialogue or self-talk. Ask a person a question and most times their eyes will move to a number of these areas. It is also said that the positions are reversed if the person is left-handed.*

These eye-accessing cues give us a clue, but not an answer, as to the person's lead or Primary Representational System, depending on the question and what their PRS is.

Say the person is right-handed and their PRS is auditory. If you ask them the colour of their front door their eyes will go to Ad first (as they ask their memory to go and recall a picture of their front door). Then their eyes will go to **Vr**. If their PRS is visual then their eyes go straight to **Vr**. Likewise, if their PRS is visual and you ask them what it feels like to get into a lovely hot bath, they would not look straight to the **K** position. They would remember an image of a steaming bath (**Vr**) and then go down right to the **K** position.

> ⇒ *Exercise:*
> *In addition to practising on friends and family, once again be observant of people being interviewed on TV. See how much their eyes move and where they are moving to. See whether you can arrive at what their PRS is and try matching it to the type of words they are using. It's a fascinating exercise*

However, the real purpose of this is honing your observation and listening skills and building your level of sensory acuity. In this regard, eye accessing cues can tell you a lot about how people process their world internally.

What other forms of sensory acuity can you sharpen to help you garner information?

> ⇒ *Look for evidence and changes in physiology, tone of voice, level of energy or animation, rate of breathing, skin tone or colour, posture and gestures. ALL these will be very noticeable, but garner and harvest the information on offer and you will have all the information you need to build rapport, then pace and lead.*

Although it is less than 10% of the communication package, always remember to notice the verbal content, by noticing the nature of the **words** that are used in description or conversation. Be aware of the person's level of articulation and react (pace) accordingly. If you are searching for just non-verbals then you'll miss the answers to your questions, and it will soon show. Set up your RAS accordingly.

It is really about opening up <u>your</u> senses and becoming a sponge for information which can be processed, and this is the goal for you in sensory acuity. Think what you are going to be using this information for: to find the other person(s) state and to fully understand and pace them you have to experience the world as they see it, by wearing their "shoes". Take a moment to translate the information you've gathered onto your physiology and detect differences in how you feel. This kind of internal pacing will give you more of a handle on how to lead others elsewhere.

Be intuitive and you'll be genuine

Practise, practise, practise at every opportunity.

> ⇒   *Set a target for every anticipated element of interaction by focusing on one particular area of non-verbal communication. It might just be to bring a smile out of the check-out girl by engaging her in such a respectful and intentional way that she is snapped out of the tedium of her job for just a moment. Try eliciting smiles from people in the street, in a relaxed and in extrovert way of course! See how good you can be by projecting your positive persona (in the form of your body language and gestures) onto others that you pass by and meet. Notice the responses, the feedback.*

VISUALISATION

In the *midst* of all this talk about noticing the senses, sensory acuity, and so on, lays the topic of visualisation. There has been a tacit assumption that you, the reader, are already well versed in this, in spite of being less well versed in all the other skills and competences mentioned here. Now I don't know whether this is so, but I am sure that by practising and improving your understanding and use of ALL the senses, you have already enhanced your abilities in the area of visualisation. You have been guided through examples of changing and switching sub-modalities and what this will bring for you and others in terms of being able to effect changes in perceptions, maps and strategies.

You now have a clearer awareness of being able to control a much more powerful mixing console for all types of creative visualisations and how they relate to training and performance, whatever the discipline.

When you read about and then create your own **"Calm Place"**, notice how real and vivid you can now make the images.

Now you can not only just use your imagination, but you can use it with diversity, elegance and ingenuity, only limited by the confines of your own creative self.

STATE BREAKERS

Having described the importance of state management in Part 1, you need to be aware of how to *break state**, whether for yourself or others. State breakers are vital because they can diffuse unpleasant or awkward situations, and also are most useful as part of anchoring, reframing and other techniques which will be explained in Part 3. A lot of work in Part 3 involves getting yourself, or others, to access a variety of different states and to facilitate the movement between these states (a breaker between each really helps speed up the process).

---

*Break state: Using a movement or distraction to change an emotional state

Using a movement or distraction to break any emotional state is a relatively simple exercise when you are guiding someone else, but is more difficult on yourself. For myself I have a preference for the "**Calm Place**", which is installed through anchoring. Mine is a vision of a wide, sandy beach where I am alone, with all the associated sounds of the beach (waves breaking, seagulls squawking) and feelings and sensual experiences of the beach (warm sun, sand between toes, light sea breeze etc). It is a multi-sensed state breaker usable on almost any occasion.

When talking to others a state breaker can be initiated by asking a question about something totally removed from the current topic. When guiding people through anchoring or reframing, the easiest thing is to ask what they had for breakfast, what they are going to do later, if they've ever been abroad or tasted Sangria? Well you'll know what to ask now I've pointed out the method.

> ⇒ *A good state breaker for pain/mild shock management is to get the person to look at their reflection in a mirror or window or something similar. Talk to them while they look at their reflection – ask them to show you where the pain/trauma/discomfort is. They will show you on themselves. Then ask them to show you where the pain is in the reflected image. As they are distracted ask who is in pain – themselves or the image of themselves. In this moment of total distraction, you can redirect their conscious*

attention to something unrelated. Perhaps ask another one or two quickfire questions. By sending their analytical conscious into overload their brain is more concerned with this area of processing than dealing with the emotional content of the pain messages.

⇒   *Another sharp state breaker is a floor-to-ceiling eye roll whilst keeping the head still. If not totally effective for self-installation, add in a power-breathe as you do it.*

⇒   *Another state breaker is to start counting downwards from 100 in steps of three.*

PRACTICAL PROJECT

Spare a thought for all the kinaesthetic oriented people. Learning or being taught skills from a V-A oriented set of text books or manuals, trying to gain competence through being taught in a language that is (at best) their secondary or sometimes their least preferred system. This might be a big project or challenge for you. Take a particular skill from your life, professional or personal, and transcribe the instructions into K-oriented language. What does it feel like now? Will it smooth some people's paths to becoming better? Will they finally be able to get a grip?

PART 3 – Fitting the Appliance

ANCHORING

Anchoring is the creating of an association to change state by setting up three triggers in **V-A-K** that you will fire at a desired moment. Anchors can be stand-alone, or can be multiple. Cases of multiple anchors are known as chained or stacked anchors.

If you look at the following example of the setting up of the **"Calm Place"**, it will give you a full insight into establishing anchors. Once you are well versed in understanding and creating anchors you will be able to soon learn and use the **"Circle of Excellence"** which will be explained later.

The **"Calm Place"** is a visualisation sequence that, once installed, can be used in a variety of ways, both as a sequence and as a snapshot to help you break state.
You need to decide upon a suitable scene for your **"Calm Place"**. It could be a beach somewhere or a leafy river bank, the choice essentially is yours. You need to make it as compelling a scene as possible, where you are the only human featured, as it is YOUR place after all.
You need to start by sitting (or lying) comfortably, and take three to four really deep, calming abdo breaths. Then use an installation script something along these lines...

> *Imagine you are lying by a river bank in a warm meadow. The sun is shining and you can feel the warmth of its rays on your skin and in your hair. Every now and then, a cool breeze whispers past the hairs on your skin like someone gently breathing your name. You can smell the fragrance from meadow flowers and grasses.*
> *You can hear some sounds. The rippling water of the flowing river*

as it dances and eddies around pebbles. Other sounds are more quiet and distant and as you lie there with your eyes closed, you can just begin to make out the sound of birdsong. You realise that the birdsong is all around you, sometimes in the air, sometimes on the ground. You open your eyes and see swallows darting through the crystal blue sky. Realising how bright and clear the sun is, you take a deep breath, let your eyes gently close again and your attention drifts back to those sounds. You can hear the wind moving calmly through the trees and the sigh reminds you of the voice of your favourite person. The breeze is drifting lightly across the meadow too and as you reach out you can feel how cool the grass is. Notice how it feels slightly damp, as grass often does, even though your back feels totally dry. The touch of the grass is so soothing on the palms of your hands, so you touch the backs of your hands to the grass and feel its coolness. You notice the way that it gently tickles the backs of your hands. Once again you press your palms into the grass and feel your fingers stretching right out as far as they will stretch.

As you hold your hands up to your face to shield your eyes from the brilliant sun, you notice the smell of the grass on your hands and it reminds you of long summer evenings at home when the smell of fresh cut grass lingered in the air. Letting your mind wander through these wonderful memories for a while, your attention is slowly drawn back to the meadow as you realise that this is the most relaxed you have ever been in your life.

Although this might not necessarily be your choice of scene, you can see how the language of the script encourages you to open up and experience ALL the senses. So when you mark out your own script, remember to get in the main three senses (visual, auditory, kinaesthetic) plus smell and taste in there as well.

Next allow the visualized scene to subside and open your eyes. Then run through this whole process three to four more times. Finally, test the installation by closing your eyes and let yourself just see one still picture of your full sequence. This will most likely be the strongest vision of your "**Calm Place**" and will be the snapshot you'll want to take with you wherever you go.

This will be the **V**isual and indeed the most powerful part of your anchor. You find you can close your eyes at any time and fire (re-create) this visual anchor.

Next, decide upon a word or phrase you will say to yourself when you want to fire this anchor. This will be the **A**uditory part of your anchor.

Finally decide upon the **K**inaesthetic part of the anchor. Let's say it is squeezing together the thumb, index and middle finger of your left hand. Using the hands for **K**inaesthetic anchoring is very common, so you need to keep a catalogue of which actions are for which anchor if you have a lot of them!

Now go through the installation sequence.

Close your eyes and see the snapshot of your "**Calm Place**" and make it bigger, brighter and bolder. When it is at its most compelling, squeeze your **K**-anchor while at the same time saying the word or phrase that is your **A**-anchor. Allow the scene to fade, or break state. Now do this sequence another three to four times. Each time make your **V**-anchor bigger, brighter and bolder.

Once this is all complete you need to break state and then test your anchors. Visualise a stressful situation in memory or coming up for you and then fire all three anchors (**V-A-K**) at once.

Judge for yourself how it worked under test. If you are happy then it is ready to use in a live situation. If you aren't convinced then fire up the Visual anchor once more and make it more compelling.

COLLAPSING ANCHORS

*Collapsing anchors** is an interesting technique, and can be described as something akin to a multi-sensed reframe. Collapsing anchors is where you have two anchors, one linked to a negative action or outcome and one linked to a positive. You use the power of the positive anchor to diffuse or counteract the power of the negative one, causing its effects to collapse. Sometimes you stack the anchors one on top of the other (making sure of course that the positive anchor is the stronger of the two) and sometimes, as in the following example, the anchors are in two separate locations but are suitably linked.

In this example relating to cricket, a batsman is backing away from the line of the ball in anticipation of quicker bowling, and we looked at how we might best help him correct this.

We anchored the approach of the quick bowler to a squeeze of the bottom hand on the bat handle, and tested the anchor. True to form, the batsman backed away.
We then asked him to visualise a less quick bowler, where he would confidently step towards the line of the ball. Once firmly established, we then anchored this to a squeeze on the top hand on the bat handle, and tested the anchor with the requisite result.
Finally, we asked him to once more visualise the quick bowler coming in and told him to <u>fire both anchors at once</u>, i.e. squeeze both hands on the handle at once. Did he step away from the ball? Answer = NO.

We tested using the bowling machine set at a speed he would have normally recoiled at, so we could see whether he would physically back away. Answer = NO. So, we were satisfied, and (more to the point) he was satisfied, that the quick bowler anchor had been collapsed.

The benefit here is that, by using the hands squeeze as the kinaesthetic anchor, any recurrence of the negative would be dealt with on a ball-by-ball basis by continually collapsing the anchor. Eventually a new positive anchor could be linked to the bottom hand squeeze on the bat handle, thus giving the player a double-positive.

This example has only dealt with visual and kinaesthetic, but we could have added auditory in there as well when we were setting up the anchors. The positive **A**uditory anchor would have been sharper, louder, better toned while the negative would have been quieter, muffled, distant. The content could have been anything associated with the visual, or perhaps more creatively, the sound of his breathing or heart beating, or cheers from the crowd as he successfully stepped towards the ball.

Sometimes, collapsing anchors can take you to the oddest places. I was at a workshop where the trainer described how a collapsing anchor routine had been set up for a competitor in high-board diving. The trouble was, the best place to set up the anchors was **on the board itself!** Not a lot of room on the 10m board for two people, plus the trainer needed to be ok with heights.

 Always with choosing and fitting the appliance, there might be several ways of achieving the same result. Your client may indicate a preference, or where the presenting problem (as for the diver) may only become manifest actually physically *in situ*.

***Collapsing anchors:** Firing a positive and negative anchor at the same time to wipe out the effect of the negative anchor

⇒ *Imagine some instances of your own where this routine might be useful or favourable. Think how you might set up the "collapse". Strategies such as these do require a bit of planning, so be aware of the time involved with installing the anchors and the choice of strategy.*

REFRAMING

Reframes are where you take an experience and re-programme the representational and emotional process of that experience. Reframes are used to replace the negative perception of an experience with a positive and mostly deal with the **V-A-K** elements of the experience.

Imagine an experience; see what you saw, hear what you heard and feel what you felt. Represent it as a multi-media, multi-sensual film. Reframes are akin to you being sat in front of a mixing console playing with the attributes of the film. The versatility of your console is considerable as it can deal with many options and variations within all five senses.

Visual reframes

Many options are available with visual sub-modalities, so you need to ascertain what the context of the required reframe is going to be. These questions need to be asked:

- Is the picture seen through your own eyes – i.e. is it associative?
- Is the picture in colour?
- Is it framed or panoramic?
- Is the contrast sharp?

- How bright is it?
- Is it moving or still pictures?
- Where in the visual field is it? Straight ahead? Left or right, up or down?

If you want to diminish the effects of a negative experience then nullify the emotional impact it is causing by:

1. Dissociating the subject. Imagine you are watching a film of yourself in the negative situation.
2. Make the picture black and white.
3. As a rule associative images are panoramic. So, put a frame around it and make it smaller.
4. Dull the contrast, make it fuzzy or out of focus.
5. Make the brightness duller or darker.
6. Make the moving pictures (the norm) into a series of stills or play with the speed.

Enhancements can be necessary and these might be:
Make it a double dissociation. Having gone to a cinema to watch this (now) black and white small screen film of yourself, if the emotion is still there then go up to the projection room in the cinema so you can see yourself in the audience watching the film.
With the picture being framed, you can make the frame as small as necessary.
Choose one still picture from the series (the one that sums up your bad feelings) and work on diminishing that. If you have a location for the image, then find if it can be moved to another location. This is particularly useful as you will see when I discuss "**Mapping Across**".

If you want to enhance a good experience into something even more compelling, just enhance all the submodalities. Make everything bigger, brighter and bolder. Play with the speed of the film to see if that will enhance the experience. If the pictures are dissociated then step into the experience.

Reframing on the hoof

There might be a particular person who is the bane of your life, perhaps someone at work. You can reframe their visual impact again by playing with the content sub-modalities. Imagine they have a clown's red nose on, or they have a melon for a head. Does that reduce their emotional impact on you?

Auditory reframes

A-reframing at the console involves dealing with sub-modalities relative to sound: volume, pitch, tone, content, repetition and location.

My favourite auditory reframe is to remove all the negative emotion from a particular voice, usually critical, which can be either internal or belonging to a particular person.
The quickest way to do this is to take the voice and then imagine the speaker has just taken a large in-breath of helium. Next listen to those critical, argumentative or derogatory words spoken in that familiar, giggly and high-pitched tone.
You can't help but chuckle and thus at a stroke the emotional impact of that voice is diminished or gone.

Here is an example of an auditory reframe I did for a young cricketer:

Many youngsters display the symptomatic stepping away from the cricket ball coming straight towards them. The ball is hard and, without protective clothing, will hurt. Plus, at some time in the past they will have been hit or seen someone else hit by a ball and experienced pain. Finding out how they represent the "stepping away" to themselves, or how they perceive what will help them, will save them, and you, hours of heartache by using a reframe.

In this example during a session on a bowling machine, the player stepped towards the line of the ball unless she identified it as coming towards her. With a straight ball, she would extricate her head and body from the danger zone leaving her hands and bat to face the consequences.

I asked her various questions to elicit which re-presentational system she favoured. I then asked her what choices she had when the ball was coming straight at her. The conversation went something like this:

Player – *I could get out of the way or I could stand and might be hit.*
PW - *What do you think will happen if you choose to get out of the way?*
Player – *I'd probably be out.*
PW – *Is that a good option?*
Player – *No.*
PW – *So what would you need to do if you were to not to move out of the way, but rather stay in the firing line?*
Player – *Hit the ball.*
PW – *And how would you get yourself to do that? What would help you?*
Player – *I'd tell myself to hit it.*
PW – *You'd hear your own voice saying, "Hit it"? You'd hear the voice inside your head?*
Player – *(Nodded)*
PW – *So, how about telling yourself that before every ball? Would that work? Imagine that now. See that ball coming at you. Keep saying "Hit it". Hear yourself say it. As the ball gets nearer are you moving to get out of the way? Is anything like that happening?*
Player – *Nothing at all.*

So we returned to working against the machine. I deliberately fired some straight balls at her to see what might happen. Not only did she NOT step away, she actually stepped across the line of the ball and tried to play it behind on the leg side. Her reaction was sheer surprise as this was something she had never done before. The way was now clear for her to move on and develop her batting without the debilitating barrier of flight from the danger of being hit.

Kinaesthetic reframes

K-reframing at the console involves working with the type of feeling, physical location and intensity of feeling.

Here's another cricketing example where during a session on a bowling machine, the player identified a scary feeling in her stomach when she perceived the ball coming at her. She said she felt this way only about deliveries she thought were going to hit her, and this made her step away from the ball.

I asked her about other types of delivery that she would happily step towards. She told me they were ones quite a way outside off stump. I then asked if she had any feelings about these particular types of ball and if so where she experienced the feelings. She said she did have feelings which were positive and confident ones and she felt these across the top of her chest between her shoulders.

I then asked her if these feelings could be moved so they could be felt somewhere else. When she said yes, I asked her to move these good and positive feelings from her upper chest down to her stomach. When she did this I then asked her how she now felt about a ball coming towards her, a ball that was going to hit her.

The reply was, "nothing at all." I asked her to really visualise it as strongly as possible but she confirmed the old scary feelings were no longer there.

The proof was when we returned to the session on the bowling machine. We watched as her feet stood firm when she faced up to straight deliveries and very soon she was playing these balls with a confident authority.

This particular reframe technique, where good, strong feelings are moved to the area where negative ones are felt, is known as "**Mapping Across**".

Mapping Across

This discipline involves taking feelings (and also sounds and images) away from one location and onto another location. The benefit here is that you can move positives into negative areas or vice versa. For people whose images/sounds/feelings are static this is less of a solution, but for those with movable associations the effects of mapping across are dramatic. People are simply amazed at what has happened. Sometimes the dynamic locations have a rotational or spinning movement, and here it is possible to reverse the movement and to experience the reframe that way. In his TV series "**I can make you thin**", *Paul McKenna*, in one programme, had his entire audience address some of their compulsive feelings by rotational reframing.

There is an example on YouTube™ with **Dr Tad James and Dr Adriana James** where they demonstrate mapping across, explaining clearly what happens every step of the way.

http://www.youtube.com/watch?v=BdqiVZ952Qo

Mapping across rather alludes to the swish pattern, and you will notice similarities as I outline the technique.

SWISH PATTERN

The swish pattern is a procedure that enables you to change modalities quickly and easily. The key point is to make the change very fast, hence the **"Swish"**. The technique usually works in one repetition; however, you can repeat the technique many times.

The procedure works like this:

Select a behaviour that you wish to change. Close your eyes and see an image of that behaviour. For example, if you wish to stop nail biting, then see in your mind's eye your hand moving up to your mouth. Actually, BE in that image and see what you would normally see. This is the cue.

Next create a picture of how things will be when you have attained your goal. For example, imagine looking at your hands and noting how good your nails look now. You feel yourself taking a deep breath and enjoying the sweet smell of success. You can make the new picture more motivating by adding in a fanfare on trumpets, flashing lights, imagining yourself standing on the winner's podium.

Now make a big, bright compelling picture of the behaviour you want to change and in the bottom right hand corner of the picture a small dark picture of the behaviour that you want.

Then in one fast reversal have the small dark image grow (or explode) to become big and bright and the old picture is overwhelmed and becomes small and insignificant (or disappears). Whilst you do this say **Whoosh** (or **Swish**) in an enthusiastic manner.

Swap the images in the time it takes to say, **"Whooshhhhhhhh"**

Open your eyes and break state.

Do the swish, four or five times and then test it to see if the old behaviour triggers the new. If not, then ensure the images are created as stated above and the swish is done extremely fast.

As stated before – **FAST IS THE KEY**

Swish is an extremely fast and effective technique to change behaviour.

I used a swish pattern (plus a bit of *timelining**) for someone to give them confidence which had eluded them every time they took a driving test. After four failures, they were keen to "buck the trend" to say the least.

We took an image of the last failed test and placed it on their timeline in the past (over the left shoulder). The image had no sound, was black and white, moving and framed and dissociated. We then went fast-forward and created an image, two months after the next test, of driving on a bright, sunny day, with friends as passengers, windows open, CD playing favourite music, no L plates on the car, etc. This was a big, bright, bold colourful associated image with good sounds, kinaesthetic pleasures etc etc and we placed it on their time-line away ahead off to the right. We then >Swished< the two images into the present – the future one growing to full panorama size and completely masking the past one which was reduced to postage stamp size. We did this four to five times and the result was a considerable change on positive feelings (a) about the next test and (b) about the emotional reaction to all the previous failures.

***Timelining:** Establishing, in a spatial sense, how and where a person represents their past, present and future.

Here's another slightly different but powerful example of swish pattern (plus) for a client with an addictive or compulsive behaviour. This swish was mixed with mapping across and some subtle positional use of visually constructed images – and so as you can see, our NLP appliances can often be used in a mix-and-match sense as best fits whatever is presenting to you.

The client had to first think of the compulsive thought or image that made him feel bad about himself. Next he had to make his right hand stiff, like a karate chop, and hold it vertically above his right thigh – like a trap door that was open over a black hole. He then had to think of the negative thoughts and intensify them as much as possible. When they could not be heightened any more, then he had to take a deep breath and blow those negative, compulsive thoughts at speed into the black hole. As soon as he'd blown them all out I would get him to SLAM the trap door shut really hard against his thigh AND immediately follow my fist with his eyes as I raised my fist upwards and to his right. As soon as his gaze reached that point I'd spread my fingers as a sign for him to take another deep breath and blow the breath away out towards the horizon.

In the course of setting up the pattern, the client not only had an image of succumbing to the compulsions but also a dark, heavy feeling in his stomach as he elicited the state. I felt it appropriate to expel everything that was being presented, so we got the feeling moving and rotating and brought it up into his mouth so that when the breath was expelled the feeling would be too.

When, a few days later, he was in a real live situation where in the past he would have yielded to the compulsions, he was more than delighted that they were no longer present. He reported the experience as "weird and uncanny".

GODIVA CHOCOLATE PATTERN

This mental pattern is a multiple derivative of swish-reframe-map across which is quite handy for dealing with situations where motivation might be severely flagging.

Take a task you have or need to do and where there is a level of reluctance or weak motivation. You know the type of task that you would utter the following phrase about:

> "I know I should but always seem to find something else to do instead"

We've all got them or needed to do at least one at some point. Next make an image of something you really, really like or love (hence the chocolate!) Study the task image and then COVER the task image with the "chocolate" image. Really study it, get into it, totally associate and remind yourself how much you love that chocolate! Intensify all your feelings. Now, in your mind's eye scratch at the centre of the chocolate image so you can JUST begin to see the task image behind it. As soon as you see it, close the hole up and re-vivify all your feelings and intensity about the good chocolate image. Do this again five times, each time revealing more of the task, each time going back to the chocolate.

At the end of this procedure, go (in reality) and view the task and see how you feel about it now. It may not be as good as the chocolate, but you should be able to get stuck into the task with a purpose and a good degree of pleasure. Taste what you see.

CIRCLE OF EXCELLENCE

This is another useful appliance where you identify a set of resourceful states you would like to take with you into any   particular situation. These states might be composure, focus, power, concentration, calmness, motivation, confidence, creativity, relaxation or indeed any state almost that you can think of.
Good sensory acuity might be one for you, or sense of humour. Accelerated learning perhaps? The choice is yours.

The process involves anchoring the desired states to stepping into the circle whilst saying a particular trigger word, and firing a kinaesthetic and a visual anchor as well. You will need to decide your trigger word and kinaesthetic anchor. Let us call them **WWWW** and **KKKK**.

Stand up and draw an imaginary circle on the ground in front of you. Size it so that if you were to step forwards you'd be at the centre and if you were to take a further step you'd be back outside the circle again. See the circle and associate a good, strong colour you'd like to take with you into this circle every time you stepped in. This would depend on the resources you wanted to take with you. A calm, relaxed colour would be different from a focused, powerful and motivated colour, or a creative colour. You need to give this a little thought, but be happy with your chosen colour.

As a primer, see the circle in front of you. See this colour in the circle, and now step into the circle and allow this colour to fill you up right from the tips of your toes to the top of your head. Feel the power that this particular colour gives you as it seeps into each and every cell of your entire body.

Now step back out of the circle and associate into your first desired state. Really get in touch with the image of this desired state. It might be a state you have had in the past. Remember everything you saw, heard and felt in that experience. Fully associate and when you cannot get any more associated, step into the circle as you say **WWWW** and fire **KKKK** and fill yourself with your chosen colour. Step back out and break state.

Next do the routine once more for your second resource state, repeating everything again as above. After this go on to the third state and repeat for however many other states you might have. (Be wary of overload) Finally test your circle of excellence by visualising, calling up or eliciting the daunting situation, scenario where you would like this stack of resources. It could be a presentation, a test or exam, a performance, even a training camp or session. Any time where in the past you've felt short of resources or a new and upcoming situation where you'd need to be at your best. Really get in touch with how you imagine it will be and as you do see yourself in the picture, fully associated, and fire the various anchors as you step into your circle and fill yourself with that colour. How does the daunting situation seem now? How do you feel about it? Have the feelings turned around? Test it and keep testing and if you aren't satisfied then go back and reinforce the areas you are less comfortable with. To put it into the plumber's context:

Plumb in the appliance → run the appliance → adjust the appliance (until happy) → finish the job

Test → Operate →Test →Exit - The TOTE model

There are some variances within the paradigm of the circle of excellence that might also prove beneficial.

I was at a workshop where the trainer asked the demonstration subject if they'd like to pick up the circle and take it with them. I watched with interest as they were instructed to "wrap up the circle" (back to the point where they had first started to draw it) and then pick it up from that one place and ANCHOR it onto one of their fingers.

"Imagine you have reduced the circle to the size of a small ring and then put this ring onto your left-hand little finger. Then whenever you want it you know it is there and you can take it off and mark out as a big circle containing all the resources you have put into that circle."

TIMELINING and FUTURE PACING

We all have a way of interpreting and processing our experiences in terms of Past → Present → Future. For some their timeline goes from the past being behind them and the future stretching out in front, for others it goes from left to right. But whatever the person and however it is laid out, we certainly all have one. Young people will find it harder to give you a description of theirs, but certainly by the time people are in their mid to late teens they have a sense of what and where their timeline is.

This is particularly useful, as witnessed with the driving test example, because you can get people to project forward. First imagining a point in the future and then getting them to see the process of moving forward from the present. I was at a workshop where the trainer illustrated this for a fighter who had an important bout coming up. He got him to fully associate into future scenes just after he had won the bout. He used the powerful feelings associated with tangible success to build into his present confidence. A confidence he knew would grow as every day he would move along his timeline.

There was a golfer who started every round he played with a calm assurance, often "birdie-ing" the first five holes. However, his game began to collapse from thereon and he would be "double-bogeying" holes in the back nine, ending up shooting well over par. By tinkering with his timeline (using NLP and post-hypnotic suggestions) he was programmed to approach every hole as if it was the first. The result being that his scores improved dramatically and his outcomes became a reflection of how good a golfer he really was.

Get to know and understand people's timelines. You can do this by just asking them, there is nothing covert about this technique. You will then use this information in setting up future pacing processes for them, rather in the way of the examples mentioned. This works both for individuals or for teams, but be aware that for teams the scripts or directions would need to be constructed to cover the varieties of positional nature of every individual player's timeline. We are all different.

Future pacing* is a technique where you shift your awareness to a time in the future and use your imagination to see what could be. It is an incredibly powerful tool that makes use of "towards" and "away" motivation. It is great for getting individuals or teams to project forward and visualise how it will be to win the trophy or execute a great performance, projecting forward to a time, after the anticipated event, and to how they and those around them will react to their success. This builds confidence and motivation in a very powerful way.

---

*Future pacing: Visualisation of 'what if' scenarios and future events for a person to observe their reaction and to test for successful change

PRACTICAL EXERCISES

⇒ *Make a list of unresourceful situations you might find yourself in. These might be areas of your game or performance which are stagnant or stuck or requiring some repair. Or (future pacing) you might want to take certain resources with you into certain situations.*

⇒ *Examine a number of ways (for each scenario) how you might best help yourself in these situations using appliances I have just listed in the catalogue.*

⇒ *You may wish to pair up with a friend or a colleague for this exercise – and practice on each other by making changes using these appliances. You will best increase your competence ONLY by experience and this is a very good way of doing so, giving as it does an opportunity to work your re-programming skills and also the outcome of improving your resourcefulness!*

ADDITIONAL PRACTICAL EXERCISES

The V-A-K QUIZ

⇒ *Score each question on a rating of 0-5 – where 0 is not you at all and 5 is your strongest preference. At the end of the quiz add up your scores for A, B and C. The mode that you score highest in indicates your preferred or lead re-presentational system: A is auditory; B is visual; and C is kinaesthetic.*

1. A. I love to listen to music.
   B. I enjoy art galleries, like window shopping, admire sunsets.
   C. I feel driven by rhythm and like to dance.

2. A. I would rather take an oral test than a written test.
   B. I was good at spelling in school.
   C. I tend to answer test questions using my gut feelings.

3. A. I've been told I have a great voice.
   B. My confidence increases when I look good.
   C. I am comfortable with and enjoy being touched.

4. A. I can resolve problems more quickly when I talk out loud.
   B. I understand things better when shown illustrations or pictorial explanations.
   C. I find myself holding or touching things as they are being explained.

5. A. I can usually assess someone's sincerity by the sound of their voice.
B. I find myself judging others based a lot on their appearance.
C. The way others shake hands with me means a lot to me.

6. A. I would rather listen to spoken word CDs than read books.
B. I like to watch TV and go to the cinema.
C. I like walking or taking part in sport and outdoor activities.

7. A. I notice even the slightest odd noise that my car makes.
B. Its important that my car is kept clean, inside and out.
C. I like a car that feels good when I drive it.

8. A. Others tell me that I'm easy to talk to.
B. I enjoy watching and observing people.
C. I tend to touch people when talking to them.

9. A. I can easily put people's voices to their names.
B. I can easily put people's faces to their names.
C. I'd rather spend time alone than go to social gatherings.

10. A. I often find myself humming, whistling or singing along.
B. I enjoy photography or painting.
C. I like cooking or making things with my hands.

11. A. I would rather have an idea explained to me than read it.
B. I enjoy speakers more if they use visual aids.
C. I'd much rather play sport than watch.

12. A. I am a good listener.
B. Its important that I always look my best.

C. I judge how I feel about someone intuitively and if I feel at ease with them.

13.
A. I always talk to myself to help me focus and deal with issues.
B. I am good at finding my way using a map.
C. Doing sport and other activities makes me feel good afterwards.

14.
A. I find it easy to imagine my favourite piece of music played on a trumpet.
B. I find it easy to imagine my front door painted purple with white dots.
C. I can remember or imagine what it would be like to sleep between silk sheets.

15.
A. I like to try to do impressions and imitate the way people talk.
B. I make a list of things I need to do each day.
C. I consider myself dexterous and well-coordinated.

TOTAL A _____   TOTAL B _____   TOTAL C _____

MOTIVATION TOWARDS or AWAY

Every action has an intention, and that action can be defined as either being towards pleasure or away from pain. Consider everything you do and it falls into one of these motivational categories.

People too become comfortable with one or other of these motivational categories and we know them as "towards people" or "away people". Towards people do their action for a positive reason (pleasure), working in the direction of a goal with a well-formed outcome. Away people are doing their action for a negative reason to get away from something, to avoid something (pain). This rather blows the "no gain without pain" argument out of the water and rightly so. The emotional barbed wire of the phrase wraps up all decent motivational thought and causes people no end of unwarranted grief. I subscribe to "no gain without effort" as no one in their right mind can be motivated towards pain.

In most cases, certainly in sport and performance, towards is the best way to be. My advice is that it is paramount you think and talk in this way and get your clients, players, the team (if appropriate) to do so too. Someone who goes training to get away from a bad atmosphere at home isn't half as motivated as someone who goes to work on their skills or fitness. So study the wording and arguments in the tests for a well-formed outcome. This should clarify all goals and underlying beliefs, for you and other people.

GOALS

In life coaching they talk about two main types of goal: **'Outcome' and 'Process'**.
You have a dream (outcome) and how you achieve that dream is the process. The dream just doesn't happen though, there has to be a plan or strategy of how to get there. This is the nuts and bolts of how the various goals will be achieved. In sports also, there is a third type of goal, **'Performance'**. This relates to measurable aspects of your own (or the team's) performance irrespective of the outcome.

Write down your goals. Put the whole thing into something tangible like a journal or diary, and get away from just a mere collection of thoughts. They then become external, in the public domain if you like, and you can view them much more objectively. You can also then apply relevant tests to them such as: are they **SMART**? Are the outcomes well-formed?

So what is the acronym **SMART**? It is a system for classifying goals. Your goals need to be:

S   Specific (not vague like "become a better person")

M   Measurable (how will you know when you have achieved your goal?)

A   Achievable (don't make it too difficult OR too easy)

R   Realistic (flyweights don't fight heavyweights)

T   Timely (set a timescale for achieving your goal)

WELL FORMED OUTCOMES

1. What do you want? State what you want only in positive terms.
2. Is it achievable? Is it a realistic possibility?
3. What will you accept as evidence that you have achieved your outcome? Let yourself know what will tell you that you have arrived at the desired destination.

4. Is achieving this outcome within your control? Or is it dependent upon the actions of someone or something else?
5. Do you have all the resources you need to achieve your outcome? These resources could be a variety of things; Money, logistical support, coaching support, emotional support, physical or mental resources.
6. What will happen when you have achieved it? Are all the costs and consequences of this outcome acceptable?

THIS IS THE ECOLOGY CHECK

The ecology check is **VITAL**, especially as working towards big goals can often throw up a number of unseen consequences which you perhaps hadn't considered and which might eventually stand in your way.

E.g.: A player wants to make the 1st team as a goal. It will give him a higher level of playing competence, perhaps some (or more) monetary reward, a sense of achievement, increased self-esteem and standing amongst his peers etc. It is achievable; he has the given ability to make it at the higher level. It is within his control; it involves further training, motivation and dedication, which on a personal level he is able and wants to give. Does he have all the resources he needs? Yes. All the costs and support are readily on hand. He has the physical and mental resources.

Ecology check: Consequences? This ambitious step involves playing matches further away, which means leaving Fridays after work and returning very late Saturdays or on Sundays. His girlfriend is unhappy as she will not see him on away match weekends, and will see him less during the week as well. She considers the situation and gives him the choice; his ambition in sport, or his personal relationship. Here the outcome is not totally well formed because he will suffer emotional and personal consequences by pursuing this goal. He needs to take further choices and considerations before proceeding.

Now this is quite a common scenario facing a lot of dedicated people, not just sportsmen and women, but how many take a look at their goals in such an analytical way? Looking at well-formed outcomes actually clarifies your beliefs and philosophies in a practical way. It is a really useful method of ensuring you have a clear pathway to every possible success. Sports and activities that regularly take you near the edges need this kind of analysis and organisation or lives will be at risk (mountaineering, caving, bungee jumping, rallying, off-piste skiing, deep sea or sky-diving for instance).

Final Question: Are you ready to begin the process? And is your unconscious mind prepared to assist in this process?

CONCLUSION

The writing of this book has been driven forward on the principle of *"if I wait for perfection I'll wait for ever"*. Rather it has been more written on the argument *"you don't have to get it right, you just have to get it going"*, a motivational catch-phrase of **Mike Litman**, a well-known success coach. So I've not strived for perfection, safe in the knowledge that there will be bigger and better opuses to follow as I gain more experience and further my knowledge of the subjects. The pursuit of excellence knows no bounds and my own quote might relate to sport but is transferable for any performance, any discipline and indeed life:

"...Excellence in sport has no beginning and no end – it IS merely about developing... No-one can ever know it all – but you can always progress – there is no such thing as the ultimate victory; everything is just a step along the way."

Peter Wright

This is one of my favourites:

> *"If you focus on results, you will never change. If you focus on change, you will get results."*
> **Jack Dixon**

And that's what this book is all about, **effecting change.**
Change in you and your thinking. Change for your team members and clients. There are many, many ways you can make a difference for them, through education, guidance, inspiration, through an infinite variety of opportunities. Hopefully I have given you some stimulus to take the subject further and enhance the richness of your experience, to the ultimate benefit of all.

There is no ultimate victory, no ultimate knowledge. Everything IS just a step along the way. This is something of a Taoist remark and so, you may well ask, the way to where?
I would say **enlightenment** is the primary target.

With interestingly curious synchronicity, I list the *Tao Te Ching* as one of my recommended reads. The Wikipedia reference on this famous work draws an interpretive comparison between its opening lines to **Korzybski's** observation *"the map is not the territory"*. I like things to come full circle as it is a universal principle, it is embodied in the *Enso* (displayed below), which we have adopted as our coaching symbol. Not just a logo, but rather an embodiment of all our working philosophies and beliefs.

I hope you enjoy mending the pipe work, installing central heating and fitting gold taps for yourself and team members as you start using your new competences. The fewer inhibitions you have, the better it will be for you and them. Every mend makes a difference and some of them are invisible being, as they are, covert suggestions and influences as a result of language.

It is said that 10% of life is what happens to us and 90% is how we choose to react to it. Your attitude determines your altitude. If you think you can, or if you think you can't, you're probably right. It all depends on your maps!

GLOSSARY of TERMS

Anchor: A trigger – visual, auditory or kinaesthetic – that links with an action or emotional state

Anchoring: The process of associating one thing with another

Associated: Being inside one's experiences and body, looking out with one's own eyes

Break state: Using a movement or distraction to change an emotional state

Calibration: Accurately recognising another person's state by reading non-verbal signals

Collapsing anchors: Firing a positive and negative anchor at the same time to wipe out the effect of the negative anchor

Dissociated: Being outside one's experience and body, looking at oneself as if on a screen or in a film

Future pacing: Visualisation of *what if* scenarios and future events for a person to observe their reaction and to test for successful change

Presuppositions: Ideas or beliefs that are pre-supposed, taken for granted and acted upon

Rapport: A relationship of responsiveness to self or others

RAS: Reticular Activating System or the brain's perceptive filter. The RAS filters out certain information gathered by the senses which is fed to the informational processing and memory areas of the brain. If this did not happen then we would go into conscious information overload – as much of the sensual information is repetitive or less relevant

Reframing: Understanding an experience in a different way, giving it a different meaning

Representational systems: The different routes by which we re-present information to our inner selves using our senses – visual, auditory, kinaesthetic, olfactory, gustatory

Submodalities: The special sensory qualities perceived by each of the senses. For example, visual sub- modalities include colour, shape, movement, brightness, depth, etc. auditory sub-modalities include volume, pitch, tempo, etc, and kinaesthetic sub-modalities include pressure, temperature, texture, location, etc

The TOTE Model: All our outward behavior is a result of these neurological processing patterns. Test – Operate – Test – Exit

Timelining: Establishing, in a spatial sense, how and where a person represents their past, present and future.

Recommended reading

You might feel that by listing the following I am endeavouring to pace and lead you towards a path *less ordinary*. Perish the thought. As you now know, there are as many ways to think of a black cat as there are to not think of one. Suffice to say, you will find my recommends either instructive, referential, amusing, inspiring, thought provoking, entertaining or just simply a good read.

Zen in the Martial Arts – Joe Hyams

Mental Training for Peak Performance – Steven Ungerleider

Blackie: The Steve Black Story – Steve Black

Tao Te Ching – Lao Tzu

Awaken the Giant Within – Anthony Robbins

The Four Agreements – Don Miguel Ruiz

Coaching with NLP – Joseph O'Connor and Andrea Lages

The Way of the Peaceful Warrior – Dan Millman

Ageless Body, Timeless Mind – Deepak Chopra

Life is not a stress rehearsal – Loretta LaRoche

Plato and a platypus Walk into a Bar - Thomas Cathcart and Daniel Klein

Meditations – Marcus Aurelius

Zen Mind, Beginners Mind – Shunryu Suzuki

Relaxing into Your Being – Bruce Kumar Frantzis

What Time is it? You mean now? – Yogi Berra

Effortless Wellbeing – Evan Finer

Training Trances – John Overdurf & Julie Silverthorn

My Voice Will go with You – The Teaching Tales of Milton Erickson

The Deep Trance Training Manual Vol 1 – Igor Ledochowski

The Magic of Metaphor – Nick Owen

NLP at Work – Sue Knight

Introducing NLP – Joseph O'Connor & John Seymour

Tricks of the Mind – Derren Brown

Winning the Mental Way – Karlene Sugarman

In Pursuit of Excellence – Terry Orlick

Grace Under Pressure: Martial arts and sports hypnosis – Adam Vile & Jo Biggs

Sports Hypnosis – Donald R Liggett

Performance Strategies for Musicians – David Buswell

Unlimited Sports Success: The power of Hypnosis – Stephen Mycoe

Pilates for Life – Darcey Bussell

Life is Short, Wear your Party Pants - Loretta LaRoche

Conzentrate; Get focused and pay attention – Sam Horn

The Way of the Dog: The art of making success inevitable – Geoff Burch

How to be a complete and utter failure in life, work and everything – Steve McDermott

Creative Visualization – Shakti Gawain

Everyday Enlightenment: 12 Gateways to Human potential – Dan Millman

Practising the Power of Now – Eckhart Tolle

The Seven Spiritual Laws of Success – Deepak Chopra

The Voice of Knowledge: A practical guide to Inner Peace – Don Miguel Ruiz

Tao of Jeet Kune Do – Bruce Lee

Winning Ugly – Brad Gilbert & Steve Jamison

Luminous Mind: Meditation and mind fitness – Joel and Michelle Levey

Wherever you go, there you are: Mindfullness meditation in everyday life – Jon Kabat-Zinn

Zen Training: Methods and Philosophy – Katsuki Sekida

Health Kinesiology – Jane Thurnell-Read

The Complete Idiots Guide to T'Ai Chi and QiGong – Bill Douglas

Unlimited Power – Anthony Robbins

Thresholds of the Mind – Bill Harris

Richard Bandler's Guide to Trance-Formation – Richard Bandler

INSPIRATIONAL ACKNOWLEDGEMENTS

Change can take a long time, but transformation takes only seconds. Some of the people below I have met, some I have seen, some I have listened to and I have read works by them all. We all have our favourite people in sport, performance, creative arts. Then we all have our **special** heroes. People who we might list as having changed our lives, sparked transformation in us, led us along new paths, affected change in **US**. Thanks to the people listed below, my life has been moved, changed, transformed by the inspiration of their thoughts, words and deeds.

Peter Shepherd	Anthony Robbins	Milton Erickson
Dan Millman	Roger Callahan	Tad James
Bill Harris	Paul McKenna	Mike Litman
Michael White	Derren Brown	Mike Brescia
Dave Alred	Don Miguel Ruiz	Richard Bandler
Joseph O'Connor	John Seymour	

And once again my thanks to Adam Vile and Jo Biggs without whose guidance and generosity I would undoubtedly be doing the laundry in the bath with a pipe wrench as a sable-coated feline looks on.

Other books by Peter Wright:

Mind How You Go
Steps to enhance your life's journey

Lamplighters
Keeping the metaphorical streets of our life well lit

Mind How You Play
Enhancing your Sporting Performance
from the Inner Perspective

Gateways to The Zone
Pathways to Peak Performance

Navigating the Ship of You
Part 1 - A Guide through Thought and Language
Part 2 – Some Chronicles of a Navigator

The Cactus Approach
Building Blocks for Invincible Teams

www.ingramcontent.com/pod-product-compliance
Lightning Source LLC
Chambersburg PA
CBHW020013050426
42450CB00005B/446